About the author

RDC is Emeritus Professor of Medicine in the University of London, UK. He was educated at Plymouth and Clifton Colleges, and spent most of his career at The London Hospital (now The Royal London Hospital, Whitechapel) and its Medical College. His main interests were internal medicine and metabolic disorders, especially those of the liver and kidneys; he is the author of many papers and chapters in books and the writer or editor of several multi-author volumes on these topics. He is the author of several monographs 'SPLANCREAS – and other offal' (2013) and 'A Muscle Odyssey' (2013), 'Man and the Liver', published in 2011, and 'NEPHROSAPIENS' (2012). Since his days as a Cambridge undergraduate he has always had a special interest in biochemical aspects of medicine. He is married to Professor Barbara J. Boucher; they have two children and five grandchildren. He and his wife retired in 1999, and now live in a small village a few miles north of Chichester, UK.

CORPUS HOMINIS

Memoirs of an academic physician

Robert D. Cohen

Emeritus Professor of Medicine
St. Bartholomew's and The London
School of Medicine and Dentistry
Queen Mary University of London, UK

Matador
9 Priory Business Park,
Wistow Road, Kibworth Beauchamp,
Leicestershire. LE8 0RX
Tel: (+44) 116 279 2299
Fax: (+44) 116 279 2277
Email: books@troubador.co.uk
Web: www.troubador.co.uk/matador

ISBN 978 1783060 672

British Library Cataloguing in Publication Data.
A catalogue record for this book is available from the British Library.

Printed and bound in the UK by TJ International, Padstow, Cornwall
Typeset in 11pt Adobe Garamond Pro by Troubador Publishing Ltd, Leicester, UK

Matador is an imprint of Troubador Publishing Ltd

Contents

*A Glossary entry is indicated by an *asterisk
in the text*

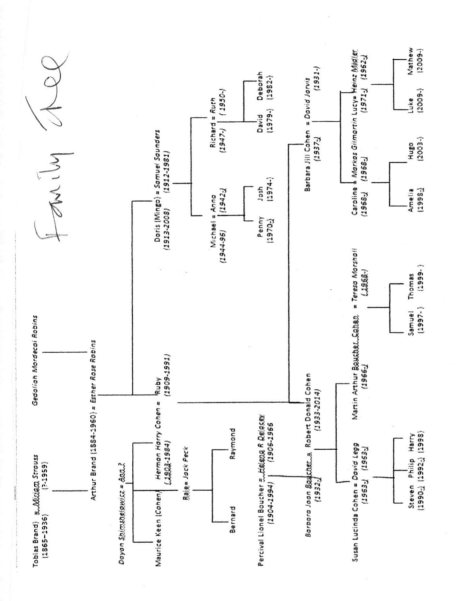

Family Tree

Chapter 1

Early life

I was born in 1933 in Plymouth, Devon, where my father, Harry Cohen, was a general practitioner. I don't actually remember the event – probably a good thing, because of the shock of emerging from a warm and cosy environment into a cold and potentially hostile world. In fact, my earliest memory was the day of my sister Barbara's birth in 1937, on which I was hustled out of the house by my nanny (Dorothy Bradburn, who lived with us until she married a Cornish farmer, Wilfred Penhaligon, when I was about thirteen), whilst the obstetricians did their stuff. I was bribed with a pair of white braces to hold up my trousers (into which I had graduated not so long previously) and taken for a walk on Plymouth Hoe. When it was safe to return home, I was taken to view the new member of the family. I was not impressed – the object was screaming its head off and had a somewhat scrumpled appearance. There was a certain amount of sibling rivalry, since my sister was somewhat spoilt. Anyone who has read the Just William books of Richmal Crompton will be aware of William's pet hate, one lisping Violet Elizabeth Bott, who always got her way by threatening to 'thkweam and thkweam and thkweam till I'm thick!' Barbara, to whom I shall refer in this book as 'Ba', her nickname, of whom more later, eventually became quite civilised! She is the family genealogist and has constructed an enormous family tree (reproduced in abbreviated form in the Appendix), starting in the 1840's with patriarchs known as Gedaliah Mordecai Robins (1848-1907) and Tobias (1865-1936) My forebears originated from Dembitz and Bialystock, cities on the Russian/Polish border.

When I was five, I was sent to a nursery school (Western College Road Preparatory School). The entrance examination mainly consisted of seeing whether I could be left for an hour or more without crying, and examining my method of descending the school staircase. The issue here was whether I could get down quickly enough in case of fire. If one used one foot after the other, without giving emphasis to either foot, this was fine; the problem was the 'dot and carry one' style of descent in which one leg always took the lead. This was inevitably slower that the preferred method, and was considered risky in case of having to evacuate the building quickly.

As might be expected, I got most of the childhood diseases (e.g. measles, whooping cough, German measles). Only one episode is perhaps worthy of comment, and this started with severe itching between the fingers. This turned out to be scabies, generally (and incorrectly) associated with dirt and poverty. It is, in fact, due to infestation with the mite *Sarcoptes scabiei*, first described by the 16th century Italian biologist Diacinto Cestoni (1637-1718), though presumably it had existed since very early times. Archaeological evidence of the disease suggests that it was present in Egypt and the Middle East as early as 494BC. The first recorded description of scabies is said to be in Leviticus, Chapter 13, verse 29. I have to say that that seems to me to be pretty conjectural since this chapter seems to be mainly pre-occupied with the diagnosis of plague and leprosy, but there are also references, e.g. verse 34, which may or may not be to scabies. The pregnant female mites burrow into the outer layers of the skin and lay their eggs, which hatch after about ten days. The symptoms are caused by an allergic reaction to mite proteins, which occur in the mite's faeces, which are deposited under the skin. The condition may be effectively treated with topical benzyl benzoate (which was the therapy I received) or, in more recent times, with permethrin or invermectin. During the war, at the height of the German bombing of Plymouth, my parents decided to evacuate my sister and me each night to a small village about ten miles north of Plymouth. We therefore caught the train each night to Bittaford, except on Sundays, when there was no service available. My parents therefore had to drive out to collect us. On one occasion my father noticed that the children of the house had scabies. From thenceforth we no longer went to Bittaford each night, since my parents regarded the horror of scabies as much worse than that of German bombs!

Plymouth had one of the oldest synagogues in the country. Whether this was because of its relatively close proximity to the village of Marazion on the south-westernmost shore of Cornwall, I don't really know. This suspicion arises because Marazion is the Hebrew for 'the bitterness of Zion', and thus it may have been here where one or more of the lost ten tribes of Israel landed. The Plymouth synagogue is built in the traditional manner, with the ladies segregated from the men in the upstairs gallery, to remove distractions, whilst the men downstairs were getting on with the business of praying. However, all this did was result in the ladies chatting to each other, with an ever increasing volume, until one of the vergers banged his hand on the reading desk and glowered at the women. One of the duties of anyone with the name of Cohen (which is the Hebrew for 'priest') was to bless the congregation near the end of the service, a task which most Cohens modestly believed they were not up to. So when the time for this blessing was nigh, all the male Cohens in the congregation, quickly got out of the synagogue, leaving one of us to peep through the keyhole of the door to let us exiles know when the danger time had passed, and we could re-enter the building.

My parents kept a large number of the Jewish traditional customs, perhaps out of respect for their local Jewish friends, rather than any profound belief in their value. Thus, the doors of our houses in Plymouth had Mezuzahs screwed on to the lintels; these tiny canisters held mini-scrolls containing the most important Jewish prayer, the 'Shema', which effectively proclaims to the nation of Israel (in the general sense) their belief in the one God. They fasted on Yom Kippur and recited a list of all possible sins that they might conceivably have committed (knowingly or unknowingly) in the previous year. These included the obvious ones – e.g. lack of chastity, bribery, evil speech, wanton glancing (!), envy, breach of trust and association with impurity, but also for any sins committed unwittingly. The scope of human misdemeanour has obviously expanded since early Christian times, when they were listed as lust, gluttony, greed, sloth, wrath, envy and pride. Though I have never actually seen it, there was also a ritual known as 'Schlag Kaporeth', in which a chicken was beheaded; the sacrificed animal was believed to bear away one's sins. On the first evening of Passover, the commemoration of the exodus from Egypt, the youngest son of the family asked the traditional question at supper: "Why is this night different from all other nights?" and was answered by the elders present, again in stereotyped fashion.

At a time near one's thirteenth birthday, Jewish boys were subject to the process of Barmitzvah, which signalled the approach of adulthood – and allowed one to be married legally in Jewish Law. On the occasion of one's Barmitzvah, you had to read in the synagogue a passage from the *Safir Torah* – the scroll of the law, whose contents were brought down from Mount Sinai by Moses, on the summit of which he received them from God. When I say "read" I mean chant, in the peculiar traditional Jewish liturgical chant. Those approaching their Barmitzvahs were carefully drilled in this chant, from books in which the equivalent of musical notes were printed under each syllable of each word. However, when it came to the actual business of singing at one's Barmitzvah, you had to read the passage from the actual Scrolls of the Law, in which the notes were absent. Since I was always incapable of singing a note except in my bath, it was lucky that my prescribed chunk to chant, which was in the Book of Genesis, was only five lines long. This was, however, only a short reprieve, since the Barmitzvah boy also had to chant a passage (known as the *Haphtarah*) from one of the Books of Prophets from the Old Testament, and in my case is was very much longer than my earlier reading from the Scroll.

During Sabbath services, members of the congregation are called up to stand beside the Rabbi during the reading of the Torah (the Scroll of the Law), the summoning is done using one's Hebrew name; mine is 'Baruch Yoseph ben Aharon Svi HaCohen', which translates as Blessed Joseph the son of 'Aharon Svi the Cohen'. So, to avoid embarrassment, you have to listen very carefully for your Hebrew name. If you by any chance miss it, the verger (known as the Shammas), comes and taps you on the shoulder, looking daggers, since your failure to comply with the summons shows that you weren't paying proper attention, or were gossiping to one's neighbour! Anyhow, I managed somehow to stumble through the Haphtarah. After the service, all present repaired to the vestry opposite the synagogue, where, accompanied by the whole congregation, one went through the service of Kiddush, in which the wine and other relevant objects were blessed. The wine was, of course, *Kosher, and, to someone who eventually was co-opted to the Wine Committee of the Royal College of Physicians, it was not really recognisable as wine! The vestry also contained the mikvah – a ritual bath in which Jewish women immersed themselves during menstruation. Orthodox Jews are not allowed to drive to and from the synagogue on the Sabbath, so they have to walk, even if they lived several miles away. My family could not put up with this, so they used to drive to a car park a short distance away, where there were many others up to precisely the same game, all trying to find room for their cars. Another Sabbath prohibition was against lighting any form of fire; this extended to the switching on of electric lights, and the orthodox used to employ a non-Jewish person to carry out these various prohibited functions on the Sabbath – a person known as a '*Shabbas Goy*'. The word '*Goy*' (plural '*Goyim*') is that applied generally to all non-Jewish persons. From the time I went to University, I dropped these various customs, not because I despised them, but because they seem to have little relevance to the modern world.

The whole business of obtaining Kosher meat was rather elaborate. This is prescribed in the Five Books of Moses. A lot of the law of *Kashrut was concerned with prohibitions, the most famous of which was not to eat meat derived from pigs, which were considered 'unclean'. This had a clear rationale in the time of Moses, because of the danger of contracting trichiniasis, of which the causative organism is the roundworm, *Trichinella spiralis*, which infests porcine muscle, and is ingested when undercooked pork is eaten – though, of course, the tribes of Israel had no idea of this fact, which was discovered in 1835 by James Paget, whilst still a medical student at Bart's Hospital. After ingestion, the larvae of the parasite penetrate the wall of the gut, enter the blood stream and set up a characteristic inflammatory reaction, consisting of swelling around the eyes, 'splinter haemorrhages' in the nails, fever, skeletal muscle pain, and, in severe cases, inflammation of the heart muscle and brain. Diagnosis is made on the basis of the clinical features, muscle biopsy to demonstrate the encysted larvae, and *eosinophilia. In the early stages, anti-helminthic drugs such as mebendazole, may be effective, before the parasite has penetrated the gut wall, but encysted larvae are not affected. Thorough cooking of potentially infected meat, or freezing at -20°C for three weeks, may prevent transmission of the condition.

Like most religions, Judaism places great emphasis on charity, and after being called to the reading of the Torah, the rabbi announced what sum of money had been donated to various charities. If one didn't want the size of one's contribution to become public, the rabbi merely announced it as a gift, which allowed one to give a pittance or a fortune without embarrassment; in my boyhood, one of the main charities donated to was the Jewish National Fund, which was devoted to funding the State of Israel, which at that time was only a concept, being formally established, amongst great and often violent protest from sections of the Arab world, by the United Nations in 1948. Those protests were answered by equally violent action from Jewish terrorist organisations such as *Haganah* and the *Irgun Zwei Leumi*. The synagogue in Plymouth had another object of charity in the local Jewish tramp. This guy had his uses; many Jewish ceremonies cannot proceed without the presence of ten or more males all of whom had been through the Barmitzvah ceremony. This minimum congregation is known as a '*minion*'. The tramp in question was present at every service, and was, in effect, receiving payment in the form of charity as a professional minion-maker. He had, therefore, to be tolerated in the synagogue, but everyone tried to sit as far away as possible from him, because he hadn't had a bath in a million years, and stank to high heaven. On leaving the synagogue after a service, it was the custom to give him a one or five pound note. When he eventually died and was undressed in preparation for burial, his disgusting coat was found to be rather heavy. The reason for this was discovered when the lining of his coat was slit up; there, stashed away, was the sum of about £4,000 in one and five pound note – no doubt the hoarded proceeds of our charity.

My own prejudice was to be extremely wary of any form of organised religion, an aspect of Mankind's history which has caused an immense amount of suffering. Examples are the death toll during the partition of British India into the present India and Pakistan, Hitler's anti-Semitism, resulting in the death of six million Jews, and endless strife between the Arab countries and Israel, since the latter was brought into being by the United Nations in 1948.

Plymouth was an interesting city. It was the central place of the Elizabethan Seadogs of Devon – Drake, Hawkins, Howard, Frobisher etc. It was on Plymouth Hoe that Francis Drake was playing a game of bowls when a courier rushed up to him with the news that the Spanish Armada, sent by Phillip II of Spain, a devout Roman Catholic, to invade England and overthrow the Protestant Queen Elizabeth I, and commanded by the Duke of Medina Sidonia (whose competence for such a role was questionable, but was nevertheless supported by the influential nobility in Spain) had been sighted. Drake gave his famous response to the effect that there was plenty of time to finish his game of bowls before dealing with the Spanish. There is a statue of Drake on the Hoe, in full Elizabethan dress and wearing his sword. The original is in the care of The National Trust at Buckland Abbey in Buckland Monachorum on Dartmoor. The drum is said to sound off spontaneously when the nation is in peril or at times of great victories. People claim to have heard the drum beating when the Mayflower left for America in 1620, when Nelson was made a Freeman of Plymouth, when Napoleon was brought into Plymouth Harbour as a prisoner and at the outbreak of the First World War in 1914. A victory drum roll was heard on HMS *Royal Oak* when the German Navy surrendered in 1918. The drum sounded off during the Dunkirk evacuation just before the outbreak of World War II, and was moved to Buckfast Abbey when Buckland Abbey was destroyed by fire. Plymouth was severely bombed in World War II (*vide infra*), a punishment said to have arisen because of the removal of the drum from its rightful home. When the drum was returned to its place of origin, the air raids ceased! A replica of the drum forms part of the base of a flagpole on Plymouth Hoe. Drake took the original drum (emblazoned with his coat of arms) with him on his circumnavigations of the globe between 1577 and 1580. All sorts of literary efforts have been based on the legend of the drum' e.g. Sir Henry Newbolt:

"Take my drum to England, hang it by the shore, strike it when your powder's runnin' low. If the Don's sight Devon, I'll quit the port of Heaven, an' drum them up the Channel as we drummed them long ago".

This poem was set to music by CV Stanford in his 'Songs of the Sea' op. 91, suite 2. Though starting in D minor, it bursts out near the end into a triumphal D major. and :-

"Drake he's in his hammock till the great Armadas come
(Capten, art tha sleepin' there below?)
Slung atween the round shot, listenin' for the drum
An' dreaming all the time of Plymouth Hoe.
Call him on the deep sea, call him up the Sound,
Call him when ye sail to meet the foe;
Where the old trade's plyin' an' the old flag flying
They shall find him ware an' wakin', as they found him, as they found
him long ago."

There is a classical jingoistic ring to these lines, typical of the Victorian age, when the British Empire was expanding, and was thought (by the British) to be the most civilising force on Earth.

Plymouth Hoe also contains the Naval Memorial, a tall white column, surmounted by a globe, and standing on a four-sided plinth on which are inscribed the names of over 7,000 sailors from Britain and Commonwealth countries who died in the First World War and nearly 16,000 in the Second World War. 'He blew with his winds and they were scattered' is carved above the names, and refers presumably to the flight of the Spanish Armada up the English Channel, around the north coast of Scotland and down the west coast of Ireland, where many were wrecked in gales.

Plymouth is on the edge of Dartmoor, a singularly beautiful area which I frequently visited as a child with my parents at weekends. Our favourite expedition was to climb a granite hill known as Sheepstor, via a variety of routes of varying difficulty. The view from the summit was spectacular, including much of Dartmoor, and Burrator reservoir which supplied Plymouth with water. On Roborough Down, the part of Dartmoor nearest to Plymouth, are sections of Drake's Leat, a stone-lined waterway built by Francis Drake with the same purpose. This leat passed under our house at 2, St. Lawrence Road, and we had to pay the City Council one shilling every year for the privilege of having a house over the leat. In the churchyard at Sheepstor village is the grave of 'The Rajah of Sarawak', actually Charles Brooke (1829-1917), who ruled as the Head of State in that part of Borneo, i.e. as the Viceroy. Towards the east of Sheepstor were the towering china clay pits at Lee Moor; to the west was Princetown, which housed the notorious Dartmoor Prison. At the entrance to this gaol was a stone arch with the words:

"Abandon all hope, all ye that enter here!"

I later discovered that this was a crib from Dante's *Inferno*:

"Lasciate speranza voi ch'entrate!"

Many years later I was driving through Princetown and stopped at this arch, lowering my window to see more clearly, when a Dartmoor pony, who was obviously used to being given sugar lumps by tourists, stuck its head through the car window, obviously looking for a similar treat. I had nothing to give it and tried to shoo it away, but it got its head stuck in the window frame. So here I was with the frightful dilemma of having a horse's head in my lap and not being able to get rid of it. Fortunately, the situation eventually resolved itself.

My father had his surgery a few doors up the road from our house. Like many general practitioners, he had a pharmacy in which he dispensed various liquid medicines, e.g. cough mixtures. He had a curious concoction he referred to as 'M+I', which stood for morphine and ipecacuanha. Morphine is well-known to suppress coughs, which seems a little odd, since the cough reflex evolved to expel sputum and foreign bodies from the airways, whilst ipecacuanha is both an *expectorant and an *emetic. Nevertheless, his patients lapped it up and were always returning for more! But what really excited me was a bottle marked 'HCN' – i.e. cyanide! This was used to settle the stomach in patients with dyspeptic symptoms; since they frequently came back for more, it must have been exceedingly dilute, in the same way as are the potions advocated by homeopaths! I used to help out by putting the large stock bottles of (e.g.) 'M+I' back on the shelves after smaller bottles had been filled for the patients to take away. It should be noted that ipecacuanha has been used by persons with anorexia or bulimia nervosa to induce weight loss by vomiting after a meal. The amount of morphine in 'M+I' was pretty small, and I only remember one patient becoming addicted to it. Her problem presented in a curious way, namely intestinal obstruction. She eventually died, and, at autopsy, her small intestine was found to be obstructed by a chalky substance. This proved to be the calcium carbonate base which the potion contained; morphine is very constipating, and no doubt the combination of chalk and constipation was responsible for the obstruction of her guts.

Turning to my days at Clifton College, the bottom end of the school playing fields (the 'Close') also housed the School's sanatorium, in which I was once confined with an attack of shingles (herpes zoster). The matron of this establishment was one Miss Clark-Kennedy, a relative of Dr AE Clark-Kennedy, one of the senior masters in the School and in my time also the Dean of the school. Shingles is caused by the same virus as is responsible for chicken pox, and usually lies dormant in the bodies of the sensory neurons for many decades until one's dotage when it suddenly erupts. That I got the condition at the early age of fifteen is a clear indication of premature senility! Because of its location, the eruption consists of a series of blisters in the line of the sensory nerve supplied by the dorsal root nerve cells in the spinal cord. Miss Clark-Kennedy told me that if the rash crossed the mid – line, I would die! So I spent a week anxiously gazing at my abdomen – the site of the rash – waiting for the expected fatal progression, which was, of course, anatomically impossible because the sensory nerves do not cross the mid-line. Years later I met this lady at some sort of reunion and reminded her of her dire prophesy. She stoutly denied having ever made it ("I would never have said anything like that!"). Herpes zoster is particularly nasty when it invades the fifth cranial nerve, which, amongst other things, supplies the conjunctiva, and occasionally causes blindness.

Of the three of us sharing a study, neither Ben Levy (who died recently) nor I were much good at sports, though we weren't bad in the rugby fives courts, and you could book one of the suite of fives courts the school provided. In contrast, Nick Tarsh was a formidable rugby football forward, and eventually got a Cambridge Blue for this sport. One of Ben's curious habits was clicking his finger joints every night before going to sleep and on awakening in the morning. The noise resembled two salvos on a machine gun; fortunately he never got round to clicking his toe joints. Ben's father was a colonel in the Royal Army Medical Corps and because of this military background Ben was expert at polishing his shoes (with spit and polish, literally) so that you can see your face reflected in the toe-caps. He also had a special mutual affinity with cats. When Ben and a cat spotted each other, they both started purring, and the noise got louder and louder, till at the moment when the cat leapt into Ben's lap to be stroked, the row was positively deafening! Ben had a lot of cat statues and models spread around his home, and introduced me to TS Eliot's Book of Practical Cats, of which *Macavity the Mystery Cat* was his favourite. He was kept under strict control by his wife, Ruth (née Shackleton-Bailey) whose father was a general practitioner in East Anglia.

I learnt two other lessons from Ben. The first was never to eat a melon in the Middle East. This was because Arab traders bored holes in melons, put them in sacks and dragged them behind their boats in the Suez Canal, which was used as a sewer by both Egypt and Saudi Arabia. The melons swelled up by *osmosis, and therefore fetched a higher price in the bazaars, and were clearly the source of numerous unmentionable diseases! The other lesson from Ben was how to cook rice, the objective being to get each grain separate, and not produce the sticky conglomerate dished up by so many restaurants. The technique was as follows: take a saucepan, put a little oil in it followed by about three quarters of an inch of rice. Cover the rice with water till there is about a further three quarters of an inch above the level of the rice. Bring the whole lot to the boil and wait till the rice has absorbed the visible water. You then take a dish cloth and wrap it around the lid of the saucepan, which is than jammed onto the saucepan, with the tea towel acting acting as a sort of sealing gasket. You then steam the rice for a further twenty minutes, remove the lid and stir the rice, which is now cooked and separated into individual grains, and may be served, preferably with curry. It is not for nothing that most food stores in the UK offer Uncle Ben's Long Grain Rice, which is, I believe, of the Basmati variety. My wife and I often eat at an excellent restaurant in nearby Petworth, named 'Basmati', which is buried in the cellars of an antique shop. The only criticism I have of UK Indian restaurants is that they frequently do not make their curries 'hot' enough for my taste, though they offer the whole range from the mildest biryani through *vindaloo* to the hottest *phal*; they appear to be slightly inhibited by the thought that the average UK citizen cannot cope with extremes of spiciness! My late father used to say that a good curry should cause sweat to run down the back of your neck!

My father, like myself, couldn't sing a note in tune, and his musical appreciation was restricted to the output of Welsh male voice choirs, singing such masterpieces as the 'Men of Harlech' and *'Sospan Fach'*. This was hardly surprising, since he was born and bred in the Tredegar/Ebbw Vale area of South Wales. Immediately after qualification, i.e. before settling down to General Practice in Plymouth, he went to sea as a ship's doctor. I still have the manual issued by the Merchant Navy giving instructions on how to deal with various diseases, including those banes of seamen, syphilis and gonorrhoea, acquired from letting their hair down in distant ports. Human immuno-deficiency virus had not yet emerged from its alleged origins in the Central African Jungle to plague Mankind, so auto-immune deficiency disease was not a problem in his ship's practice.

Standing on Plymouth Hoe and looking out to sea over Plymouth Sound, one can see the breakwater about three miles offshore, which contributes to the excellence of Plymouth as a harbour. Just inshore of it is the breakwater fort, and seawards to the right is the Eddystone lighthouse. On a clear day, a curious stump-like object is visible next to the lighthouse and situated on the same rocks. This is the remains of the original lighthouse, which was dismantled and brought brick-by-brick to Plymouth Hoe, where it was reassembled, and is now known as Smeaton's Tower, after its original builder. Inside the tower is a spiral staircase which takes one to the lamp housing. There are magnificent views from the top of the tower. Looking out to sea, on the right is the exit of the River Tamar; upstream are the naval docks at Devonport, and I used to be thrilled by the appearance of all types of naval vessel, including, best of all, submarines! Further up the Tamar, one comes to the Torpoint ferry, which used to be the sole convenient means of crossing the Tamar into Cornwall, until much more recently, when a suspension bridge was built, allowing one to drive into Cornwall straight from Devonport. Until this bridge was built, the queues for the ferry were so great that it was sometimes quicker to drive up the east side of the river until, after ten to fifteen miles, one reached the village of Gunnislake, where there was a bridge over the river, which is much narrower at that point.

Returning to the Hoe, and looking this time eastwards, there is an extension of the Sound into the Barbican area, which is where the fish are landed from small boats. Fresh fish may be had from the fish market, where local fishermen are seen gutting their prey. The smell is interesting, because of the failure to clean up properly at the end of the day. In a backstreet near the Barbican is a well-preserved Elizabethan house. On the east of the Hoe is the Citadel, with ancient cannon protruding through the ramparts, and much more importantly, the world-renowned Marine Biological Laboratory. This boasts an aquarium, much beloved of small children, who are terrified by sharks, crabs and lobsters of menacing appearance. When I was at Cambridge, my tutors Alan Hodgkin and Andrew Huxley, who won Nobel Prizes for their work on nerve conduction, used to visit this laboratory frequently, since the fisherman brought in a plentiful supply of squid. It was on the squid *giant axon (each animal has two of them) that Hodgkin and Huxley did their fundamental work. Huxley was also responsible for working out the reason for the segmented *myelination of motor and sensory nerves. The segments were separated by very small intervals at which the plasma membrane of the nerve fibre was exposed. These were called the Nodes of Ranvier. This feature allowed the action potential to leap from one node to the next, without having to laboriously depolarise the complete length of the nerve fibre membrane. This process was known as saltatory conduction, and greatly increased the speed of conduction in myelinated nerves compared with that seen in unmyelinated nerves, such as those of the sympathetic nervous system. It is possible that part of the disability caused by demyelinating diseases such as multiple sclerosis is due to the slowing of conduction.

In the eastern distance is the promontory of Stadden Heights, which is topped by a characteristic wall. I have no idea what this wall was built for, though there is some sort of fort beneath it. On the plateau of the Heights is a golf course, principally remembered by me because my maternal grandfather, Arthur Brand, had a heart attack just under the wall, which he fortunately survived. My late friend, Ben Levy, always described golf as 'a good walk spoilt', wondering why some people couldn't take a walk without beating the living daylights out of a small white ball! Arthur Brand, my maternal grandfather, was the proprietor of four electrical shops in Plymouth, two of which were on a sunken plateau known as Mutley Plain, so named because in previous times it was the site of a lunatic asylum, or 'motley house'.

I had a great-grandmother still alive in Plymouth, who was by that time bed-bound, and I was occasionally taken to visit her. Other relatives in Plymouth ran pawn shops, no less, equipped with the characteristic sign of three balls. One of them was graced with the somewhat pretentious name of 'Manchester House', but in fact it was a good honest pawnshop.

At about the age of five, I was moved from the infant school to the local primary plus secondary school, Plymouth College. This was made respectable by the fact that it belonged to the Headmasters' Conference of Schools, which included Eton, Harrow, Winchester and the like. I don't remember too much about Plymouth College, except that, since I was quite bright, I kept on being moved up a form or two, so that my classmates were always older than me and I was bullied unmercifully by them. There was a mathematics master by the name of Bonser, and a chemistry master called Eric Holman, who used to stare at me in disgust, and say "I like a manly man and a womanly woman, but I can't stand a boily boy!" My guess was that he also suffered from acne as a teenager, and was simply taking retrospective revenge. In practical chemistry classes we used to make ammonium nitrate on the quiet; this substance is highly explosive, and goes off with a bang on the slightest touch. So we used to put it on the radiators – where it exploded spontaneously and sprinkle it on the floors so that during the chemistry master's perambulations whilst teaching, his words of wisdom were continuously interrupted by mini-explosions. There was a paternoster-type lift connecting the chemistry laboratory to the physics laboratory on the floor below. We used to drop ammonium nitrate down the lift shaft so that physics lessons were also disturbed by explosions. For indiscipline of one sort or another, you were caned, the number of strokes being decided by a 'Star Chamber' of prefects. On one occasion, I remember returning home after receiving two strokes, admiring the weals on my rear end in a mirror; they were parallel to each other and separated by about a quarter of an inch, attesting to the accuracy of the prefect administering the punishment. We had a German teacher who had escaped from the Third Reich, who attempted to keep discipline by the use of a curious cane with a knob on the end with which to grasp it. We used to throw paper aeroplanes constructed from sheets of paper at each other during German lessons; on one such occasion when I was caught in the act he brandished his cane at me saying "Cohen, the next time I catch you doing ziz I vill haf to beat you!" Plymouth College had a French teacher who was engaged to coach me for the Winchester entrance scholarship examination, and who suffered from severe Besnier's Prurigo. This condition consists of eczema, principally in the flexures of the elbows and knee joints, but in severe cases covers the body and causes intolerable itching. The sufferers scratch desperately to try to relieve themselves and my poor French master always walked around in clouds of displaced flakes of skin.

At this age I was fascinated by the whole business of explosions, and used to make gunpowder from potassium nitrate, sulphur and iron filings in the top room of our house in Embankment Road. A large pinch of this concoction was then placed on a metal block and hit by a hammer; the resulting bang used to terrify my mother. We were also not very fond of the people next door, so we used to make paper aeroplanes, set them on fire and throw them out of the window, thus setting the neighbour's hedge on fire!

The next event of any note was the outbreak of World War II. We were on holiday in Bournemouth when this happened, and I remember listening to Neville Chamberlain's radio address, telling us all that we were at war with Germany. My memories of the war are dominated by the fact that Plymouth was heavily bombed from 1941 for a year or more. We were woken at night by the warning sirens, and immediately repaired to our concrete air-raid shelter, which my parents had had constructed in our front garden. There were two sorts of air-raid shelters, the concrete shelter and the Anderson shelter, which seemed to be to be little more than a dugout covered by sheets of galvanised iron and earth. Both these shelters provided some protection against flying shrapnel and debris from bomb explosions, but neither would save one from a direct hit. Until he was called up into the Royal Army Medical Corps, my father used to receive casualties in our shelter and dress their wounds as well as he could. Perhaps this helped to initiate my interest in Medicine, though more of this later. After the all-clear was sounded we emerged from the shelter to inspect the damage. I remember at the height of the Blitz the whole sky over Plymouth was reddened by the flames below. But the great excitement for us children was to rush around the streets collecting shrapnel and the tails and nose cones of incendiary bombs, which we used to swap at school with whatever the other boys had collected. The main body of the incendiary bomb, of which there were many specimens lying around the streets, had a peculiarly nasty smell, presumably arising from some sort of phosphorus compound. Almost every house in Plymouth had its windows shattered by bomb blast, and we used to protect ourselves against flying glass by covering the panes with a criss-cross pattern of sticky tape.

The other pre-occupation of small boys at that time was the game known as conkers. I have no idea if this is still played, but, in case it is not (due to excessive 'Health and Safety' fears), here is some information which readers' children may find irresistible. A conker is a horse chestnut, so they may only be collected in autumn, when the chestnuts are shedding their seeds. The first thing to do is to pierce the conker with a skewer, the tip of which has been heated till red-hot on a gas ring. A piece of string is then threaded through the hole, and a knot tied in one end so that the conker may be either dangled or swung. One of the two players takes the active role and tries to smash the other's dangled conker. If he succeeds, then his conker is known as a 'one-er'. That successful conker acquires all the scores of the conkers that it has smashed; thus if it smashes a 'fiver' and a 'niner', it is now a 'fourteener'. After a 'miss', i.e. no damage has been done to the opponent's conker, then the active role is taken by the other player. There are two useful ways of cheating; firstly, you can (apparently accidentally) miss, and bash your opponent on his knuckles, which is exceedingly painful, causing either tears or blasphemous utterings. Secondly, you can bake your conkers in the oven before stringing them, which makes them very hard.

In 1941 my father was called up into the Royal Army Medical Corps (RAMC) and was first stationed at Leeds. This posting always meant that the individual concerned was shortly to be sent overseas. Families were not told where their loved ones were to be posted, for obvious security reasons, and any place names found in letters from members of the armed forces were excised by the censors. However, my parents had devised a code so that my mother would know pretty exactly where my father had been posted. It was thus that my mother got to know that my father had been posted to a gigantic camp in Kenya, for members of the King's African Rifles who had contracted venereal diseases! At this time venereal diseases comprised mostly *syphilis and *gonorrhoea, since human immunodeficiency virus had not yet evolved from its simian counterpart (SIV) in Central Africa. Human Immune Deficiency disease was thus a thing of the future, and genital herpes and chlamydial disease had not yet been recognised as venereal diseases. However, by this time *syphilis no longer had to be treated with arsenical preparations such as Salvarsan, and both syphilis and gonorrhoea were still susceptible to the increasingly available penicillin, which had been discovered accidentally at St. Mary's Hospital in London by Alexander Fleming and developed for mass production by Ernst and Chain at Imperial College.

When my father arrived in Kenya he was sent to Thika, which housed the centre for treating the venereal diseases referred to above. Immediately on arrival, he was summoned to the Commanding Officer's office, who said to him

"Lieutenant Cohen, you haven't got a gun, have you'.
To which he replied "Of course, I have – standard issue!"
The CO took alarm, and shouted:
"Well, give it to me at once – mustn't have things like that lying around!"

My father was mystified, since he thought that the whole point of being a soldier was to have a gun with which to defend oneself. But he handed over his lethal weapon, and the CO immediately threw it down a deep dark pit. It turned out that he was dead scared of the local natives filching it, as well they might have, even though the Mau Mau uprising was yet to come. When my father was later posted back to the UK, the CO restored his pistol to him, and I later found it in our box room at Embankment Road. My mother found me trying to load it with ammunition. Not surprisingly, she panicked and took the pistol to the local army depot on the outskirts of Plymouth.

My father, meanwhile, decided to explore the facilities in Thika. One day he looked over the boundary wall of the camp and saw a lot of natives lying around with extensive lesions resembling those of smallpox and he rushed off to the CO to tell him of this dire discovery. The CO just yawned, pointing out that this was not true smallpox but an attenuated form of the condition known as alastrim. Whilst at Thika, he met another RAMC physician whose surname (I forget his given name) was Maxwell and they became good friends. They went on local leave together and visited a pygmy village near Kilimanjaro. Here my father bought a pygmy bow and a quiver of arrows, which he sent home to me, and I proudly displayed this trophy to my school mates. Another trophy arose because a plague of locusts suddenly appeared in Thika. You could simply knock large numbers of these creatures out of the sky by waving your hands around. So, one day a package of dead locusts arrived at home, which I kept for many years before they disintegrated entirely.

Whilst at Thika, my father got a sudden attack of renal colic. This was due to an attempt by his urogenital system to pass a calcium-containing stone. X-ray investigations in Nairobi showed that he had the condition known as 'horseshoe kidney', in which the lower ends of the kidney are joined together over the front of the spinal column at the back of the abdominal cavity. The ureters, which are the tubes connecting the kidneys to the bladder, pass over the front of the fused lower poles of the kidneys and in the process tend to get obstructed. The combination of this partial obstruction and dehydration due to the warm Kenyan climate create the ideal conditions for stone formation. The discovery of this condition caused my father to be returned to the UK and demobbed, since the Army obviously could not be expected to put up with this sort of condition, the stones being highly likely to return. The only downside to my father's premature return from the war was that it deprived me of receiving any further trophies, such as those described in the last paragraph! My mother, sister and myself met him at Plymouth Railway Station, where at first we didn't recognise him. This was because his skin had a deep yellow colour due to his having had to take mepacrine as an anti-malarial. However, his erstwhile patients in Plymouth were delighted at the return of their favourite GP – which brings me to what happened to his practice while he was away at the wars. My mother had engaged a locum to take over the practice, and I remember the tremendous kerfuffle when it was discovered that this man was an imposter and not a registered medical practitioner at all! He was swiftly removed – I am not sure whether police action was taken against him. Anyhow, he was replaced by a retired doctor, who was indeed on the medical register. He had, however, one particularly nasty habit, which was that at meal times (he lived with us) he took out his false teeth and placed them on the table! My mother, however, decided that she would have to put up with this.

After the war, my cousin Bernard Peck (son of my father's brother, Maurice) became my father's partner and came to live with us in Plymouth, sharing a bedroom with me. He had a strong aversion to onions, so one day I dangled an onion from the light-pull just above his nose. When he woke up he was confronted by his pet hate! He was an excellent painter, being particularly adept with the palette knife, and I have one painting of his, a village scene in France painted after the manner of Camille Pissarro. He married a girl from South Wales named Pat Fligelstone, but tragedy struck when they were on vacation driving through the Pyrenees near the small town of Puigcerda, when they were attacked by a bandit, who shot Pat dead and severely wounded Bernard in the neck. He was found and taken to a local hospital, where they patched him up and the Spanish authorities flew him back to Cardiff in a chartered plane. I well remember waiting for the plane to arrive; when it did, Pat's coffin was taken out of the hold of the plane on to the shoulders of pall bearers.

Shortly after his return home, my parents decided that Plymouth College was not the best place for me, so they set about trying to find some other school. Firstly they tried Winchester College; here the scholars ate off wooden trenchers. The technique was to build a continuous rampart of mashed potatoes around the edge of the square trencher. You could then pour the gravy and other constituents of the vile stews the boys were fed into the protected central space. The square trenchers, of course, gave rise to the concept of 'a square meal', which is of naval origin and refers to their use by crews in the cramped space of the ships' galleys. Because of the square shape of the trenchers, you could fit more sailors on to a bench than if the food was served on round plates. Fortunately, I failed the entrance exam dismally, principally because I had no knowledge of Greek!

Winchester Cathedral is a good Gothic building, distinguished for containing the grave of Jane Austen (1775-1817), my favourite author. The next school my parents tried was Westminster; I have not much to say about this educational emporium, except that the boys had the privilege of shouting "*Vivat, vivat, vivat*" at coronation services in the Abbey. The school where I finally ended up was Clifton College in Bristol, which my parents rather fancied, since it had amongst its residential houses the establishment known as Polack's House, which took Jewish boys exclusively. The history of Polack's House is recorded in detail in a book by Derek Winterbottom[4] entitled "*Dynasty*". It starts with a certain Lionel Cohen (no relative – the world seems almost as full of Cohens as it is of Smiths). Lionel Cohen was an authority on the organisation and financing of railways and was instrumental in the setting up of the Board of Guardians of British Jews, which then gave charitable help to Jewish immigrants fleeing from persecution in Russia, Poland and Romania. It is salutary to reflect on this predecessor of the flight of Jews from Nazism in the 1930's; in brief, in 1875, the Chief Rabbi wrote to the then Headmaster of Clifton, the Revd. John Percival, proposing a Jewish house; he put it before his Board of Governors, who initially rejected the idea, but were later persuaded by Percival to accept the idea. It is no coincidence that Polack's was situated in Percival Road, Clifton, a few hundred yards from the main campus of the school. I actually rather enjoyed the entrance examination, at which the prospective new boys were taken around the campus by the school librarian, one Mr. Stedman, who had a pronounced limp, causing him to walk, leading with the same shoulder all the time. At one of our rest stops on our tour of the campus (known as 'The Close'), I casually remarked to Mr. Stedman that really we were being assessed by him as possible pupils. Curiously, he thought that this was a remarkable piece of insight, and this may have been one of the reasons why I got the top scholarship of the year to Clifton. The view of Clifton from the far end of the Close was quite attractive, and was the inspiration for Henry Newbolt's famous lines:

"There's a breathless hush on the Close tonight
Ten to make and the match to win
A bumping pitch and blinding light,
An hour to play and the last man in.
And it's not for the sake of a ribboned coat,
* or the selfish hope of a season's fame,*
But his Captain's hand on his shoulders smote –
Play up! Play up! And play the game!"

I must now say something in more detail about Polack's House, which was one of the main reasons why my parents eventually sent me to Clifton. Polack's House was thought to be the best compromise for a Jewish boy between being sent to a school where all the pupils lived in mixed establishments, regardless of faith or the religion of their parents on the one hand, and a totally Jewish school such as Carmel College, where there was no opportunity to meet with children of different 'inherited' faiths. There was, at Clifton, very little of the sort of apparent anti-Semitism of Hilaire Belloc:-

"How odd
Of God
To choose
The Jews!"

To which the obvious response of many Jews was:

"It's not so odd –
The Jews chose God
Because the Goyim
Annoy 'im!"

For generations the Housemaster had been a member of the Polack family. When I was there, the Housemaster was Albert Polack. He was followed by a cousin, Philip

Polack, a modern languages teacher, and later by one of Albert's sons, Ernest. After Ernest, the Polack line ended, and he was succeeded by a non-Jewish Housemaster. The history of the Polack family has been recorded in a book by Derek Winterbottom*. Polack's House had a small synagogue, at which the Housemaster officiated on Saturday mornings. Because the rest of the school had classes on Saturday, the Polack's boys had an extra class on Sunday mornings to make up for the teaching time lost on Saturdays. The Polack's boys ate with the rest of the boys in the Great Hall, where they received allegedly Kosher food. You queued up bearing your plate at the serving counter for the chief cook, known unaffectionately as 'Ma Butch', placed an inadequate dollop of some indeterminate stew on your plate. A few boys had the temerity to ask for more, or go up for a second helping, like Oliver Twist at Dotheboy's Hall. I remember the occasion when a dead mouse was found in the stew – quite tasty! It was not surprising that I sent urgent letters home, claiming that 'starvation reigns', which resulted in food parcels being dispatched by my worried parents.

At Polack's House, each boy had a study, shared with two, three or four other pupils. My first study was shared with my life-long friends (to whom I have referred earlier) Nick Tarsh (Derek Nicholas Tarsh) and Ben Levy (Benjamin Keith Levy), who died recently. For a short while we were joined by Alan Denman, with whom I later edited a book ("*The Metabolic and Molecular Basis of Acquired Disease*"). The purpose of the study was a place to keep one's books and to do homework. But they were also places where the aforesaid food parcels were opened and their contents avidly consumed. Thus they accumulated wrapping paper and empty tins of this and that, and so became pretty disgusting. They were inspected weekly by the housemaster. From the window of the study you could see a playing field and the toilets, which were in an outside block. The latter was unheated and one often endured the slings and arrows of outrageous constipation rather than freeze to death in the toilets. Ben also had a good story about 'The cat that crept into the crypt, crapped, and crept out again' (rather a good tongue-twister)! Ben married Ruth Shackleton-Bailey, daughter of an East Anglian General Practitioner. Finally, to improve our social accomplishments, Clifton College arranged dancing classes with the girls of Clifton High School for Girls. Ben took a dim view of dancing, describing it as 'an upright representation of a horizontal desire'! One of the things I did, on one of Ben's cats, was to look into its eyes with an *ophthalmoscope. The back of a cat's eyeball is a brilliant green, in contrast to a similar region in the human eyeball, which is reddish-orange. Furthermore, in humans, the branches of the retinal arteries emerge together from a circular depression – the optic cup – in the middle of a clear white disc, whereas in the cat, they emerge separately, at equally spaced points on the circumference of the disc. My interesting observations were cut short when the irate animal stuck out a paw, and scratched my face!

During most of my four years at Clifton, the Headmaster was Basil Hallward. He was a classicist (of course) and once said to my sixth form class "Boys! You know why Sparta declined? You don't! Well, I'll tell you. It was buggery, sheer buggery!" Hallward later departed for the scene of my previous failure, Winchester, where I hope that the boys benefitted from his wisdom. Clifton had strict ideas about the arrangements in the sixth form. The cleverest boys went into the Classical Sixth, the next grade of intelligence to the Modern Languages Sixth and the third level to the Mathematical Sixth. Those of only minor intelligence went to the Science Sixth, whereas the real idiots were condemned to the Military Sixth, despite the fact that the armed forces had been responsible for saving us from the Hitlerian scourge in World War II. Having got a scholarship to Clifton I was naturally directed to the Classical Sixth, which was not at all to my taste and I threatened to run away. After a good deal of haggling between the school, my parents and myself, I was eventually put into a class known as The Remove (? a dustbin for awkward characters). The form-master was the Reverend Oliver Grove, known to the boys as the Holy Grove, who was indeed a classicist, but a couple of days a week I was allowed to go to science classes, which allowed me to retain my sanity. These classes included physics, chemistry, botany and zoology. One of my unsuccessful enterprises was an attempt to measure the velocity of light down the long corridor of the Science Building. In fact, I have always been grateful for the modicum of Latin that was drummed into me at Clifton, since this language, 'dead' as it is, was a great help to me in my future readings and writings. When one had graduated into the Sixth Form, there was a good chance of becoming a prefect (known at Clifton as a 'Praepostor'). You then had the privilege of walking around the campus with your hands in your pockets, but you also had to administer discipline – for instance – punishing boys who did the same, or failed to doff their school caps when passing through the Memorial Arch at the entrance to the main part of the campus.

Like many young men of an academic bent, I became interested in philosophy. My 'bible' was Bertrand Russell's *"History of Western Philosophy"*[1] which I was given as a prize for coming top of my division of the Sixth Form. I was particularly interested in the views of a cleric, George Berkely (1685-1754), who maintained that objects only existed through being perceived. Russell gives the example of a tree, the thinking about which inspired a limerick by Ronald Knox, which I reproduce here:

"There was a young man who said, "God
Must think it exceedingly odd
If he finds that this tree
Continues to be
When there's no one about in the Quad"".

To which the reply was:

"Dear Sir,
Your astonishment's odd
I am always about in the Quad
And that's why the tree
Will continue to be,
Since observed by
Yours faithfully,
GOD"

During my time at Clifton, my parents often took my sister Ba and myself on holidays abroad, often to various parts of France, which, not surprisingly, were generally in a somewhat dilapidated condition, having only recently been rescued from the depredations of the Wehrmacht. We used to book in for the night 'on spec' in a likely-looking hostelry, the only precaution taken before committing ourselves being my mother ensuring that meals would be served without contamination by garlic, which she and her parents had been brought up to consider as the food of the Devil (curiously, the flavour of garlic is largely due to the to the presence of mercaptans, organic sulphur-containing compounds, which would have certainly met with Luciferian approval). Notwithstanding assurances on this point, the meals were always served reeking with garlic. The reason for this eventually became apparent. My mother thought that the French word for 'garlic' was actually 'garlic' (whereas it is, in fact, '*ail*') and her request was phrased '*pas de garlic*', which merely mystified the restaurateur!

The first of our overnight stops on one such trip was in the town of Arras, the capital of the Pas de Calais administrative department in Northern France. The hostelry was the Hotel Brasserie Moderne and we had three rooms, one for my parents and one each for Ba and myself. When I got into my room and started to unpack, I opened the wardrobe and found it to contain a half-chewed crust of stale bread, obviously part of the meagre rations allotted by the Germans to local inhabitants. The next morning, I got up, knocked on my parents' door and the door panel immediately fell in! My parents leapt up in consternation, thinking they were being attacked by vandals!

Our journey continued in a south-easterly direction to our next stop, Chalons-sur-Marne, and we booked into the Hotel Haute Mère Dieu. The next stop was Contrexeville, just south of Nancy, then Vittel and Évian-les-Bains on the south shore of Lake Geneva. All these were spa towns, where invalids from around the world congregated to imbibe the allegedly health-giving waters. There is, of course, no evidence for the curative effects of any of these waters, except in the negative sense that none of them contained alcohol. Some of them stank and tasted of sulphur, which fostered the widespread notion that the nastier the medicine, the more potent it is. Some spas even advertised themselves as '*sources radioactifs*', fostering the idea that a bit of radiation was good for you! As far as we were concerned, the only potable one of these products was Évian, so we thereafter stuck to this one on our travels. We eventually crossed the border into Switzerland at Basel, and the contrast between the rich, tidy and glittering aspect of this country (which, of course, was not involved in any military sense in the war) compared with the drab, dirty and run-down France was all too obvious. Basel is situated on the bend of the Rhine, as it turns north to Freiburg-im-Breisgau after flowing out of Lake Constance. Many years later, I attended a conference in Basel at the headquarters of the pharmaceutical company Hoffman La Roche. The seats in their conference room were magnificently equipped with a series of buttons on the left hand arm rest. One button signifies to the Chairman of the session via his own panel, and also the speaker at the lectern, that you want to ask a question. Another button lit up to amplify the speaker's reply in your headphones. There was a third button whose function was a mystery to me, but may have been used to open a trapdoor under the speaker, dropping him into the Rhine if you thought he was talking rubbish! I once stayed in a hotel in Freiburg, a city where Hans Krebs once worked. When I got home, I found that the sports coat which I had been wearing was missing. It turned up by post a few days later, freshly laundered! Most hotels of the world would just send it back in its original state, but the German and Swiss hotels tend to be obsessively clean, and I was often struck by their smell of furniture polish! On one occasion, when I was a student at Cambridge, I was travelling by train from The Hook of Holland to Basel, and fell asleep; when I woke, we seemed to be travelling back to the Hook again – much to my consternation! It took me some time to work out what had happened. When the train reached the town of Mainz, it firstly passed it to the east, then, having passed it, it turned west, and then north into the station. At the platform, the engine is uncoupled from the train, and another engine reverses on to the back end of the train, and is there coupled to the carriages. It is this second engine which takes the train to Basel, and that was the reason for my illusion of travelling in the wrong direction! On this journey, before reaching Mainz, we passed through the city of Cologne, or at least what was left of it after the attentions of the Royal Air Force during the War; in fact, the only thing that appeared to have been left intact was the Cathedral, either due to the accuracy of RAF bomb aimers (or, possibly, to Divine intervention!). On this journey, I was so strapped for cash that I existed virtually on bread and peaches for the whole ten days.

Another of the conferences I attended was in Prague, accompanied by my colleague Bill Asscher. We travelled by train to Czechoslovakia, and, when we reached the Czech border, Russian army officers demanded our passports at gun point. We spent an anxious fifteen minutes, now being effectively stateless persons likely to end up in the Gulag. Adding to our fears was the presence of armed guards on the opposite side of the train to the platform, making sure we couldn't escape by that route! Eventually, however, our passports were returned and we proceeded on our way.

Returning to our first trip to Switzerland, one of the first stops after crossing the border from France was Freiburg-im-Breisgau (*vide supra*). We ended up at the Hotel Schweizerhof in Lucerne which, at that time at least, seemed palatial. The lake at Lucerne is the Vierwaldstättersee, so-called because it has shores bordering on four wooded cantons. My sister 'Ba' and I greatly enjoyed swanning around on the lake in the curious pedalos, which, as their name suggests, were powered by pedalling. The lake cascades into the Rhone under an extremely ancient, roofed, wooden bridge, which has murals painted on its ceiling. Along the lake there is a promontory with a small chapel – *Tellskapelle* – which is the point where William Tell, according to legend, leapt ashore from the boat of his captors, servants of the tyrant Gessler, whom he later assassinated. Tell's exploits eventually led to the foundation of the Old Swiss Confederacy. Lucerne had then, and still has now, innumerable Swiss watch shops, containing timepieces which have, in addition to a clock, many other functions, e.g. giving information on the phases of the moon, high and low tides and the altitude of one's present location. The downside of this industry in its earlier days was the habit of the watchmakers to point their brushes with their mouths when painting on the luminous paint, which contained small amounts of radioactive phosphorus. This habit resulted in bone necrosis, malignant bone tumours and fractures of the jaw, a syndrome known as 'phossy jaw'. Lucerne is surrounded by three mountains, the two highest being Mount Pilatus (height 2132 m), which I and the family have ascended by mountain railway, and Mount Rigi. We have a striking watercolour of sailing boats on Lake Lucerne, near the village of Brunnen, done by Edward T Compton (1849-1921).

Another of my favourite Swiss haunts was Interlaken in the Bernese Oberland, situated between Lake Thun on the west and Lake Brienz on the east. There are magnificent views of the surrounding mountains – the Jungfrau (4,158 m), the Mönch (4,107 m) and the Eiger (3,970 m). We ascended this mountain group by means of a remarkable rack-and-pinion railway, opened in 1912, which is tunnelled through the Eiger. There are various stops on the way up, the platforms having openings on to the north face of the Eiger (the Eigernordwand). If you look out of these openings you can see numerous items of equipment, e.g. pitons and ropes, left behind by those attempting to climb the North Face; this is apparently one of the severest challenges in the world of mountaineering. At the top of the railway, on a plateau known as the Jungfraujoch, there is a restaurant and observation platform, from which there are superb views of the Aletsch glacier and for hundreds of miles north and south – providing you chose the right day for the trip! At this altitude, we were all distinctly breathless on exertion.

The road on the side of the Vierwaldstättersee passes through the Axenstrasse, a remarkable series of arches cut into the mountainside and, eventually, reaches the foot of the St. Gotthard Pass, the top of which is about 7000 ft above sea level. At Göschenen you have the option of driving over the pass, snaking through an enormous number of hairpin bends, or getting your car put on a train that takes you through the St. Gotthard Tunnel. Both the road over the pass and the train come together again at Airolo, in the Italian speaking part of Switzerland. The car mechanic who was unloading my grandparents' car from the train grabbed the handbrake handle, but clearly didn't know how it should be operated in Daimlers. He started waggling it to and fro with increasing force and eventually the whole thing came off in his hand. The mechanic shouted *"Ach, Christo!"* which was my first experience of Italian expletives. However, some sort of repair was cobbled up and we were able to continue our journey. On another family visit to Switzerland we went to Zermatt, at the foot of the Matterhorn. There were magnificent views of the mountain from our hotel, which I painted (Plate 1) and the village had a monument commemorating the first ascent of the mountain by Edward Whymper. Only two of the climbing party of four came back alive, owing to the leading guide slipping on the way down. Whymper and a colleague had desperately tried to save their colleagues who had slipped, but the rope broke, and the two leading members of the party fell to their death. Some accused Whymper of actually cutting the rope to save himself from being pulled over, but there was nothing to substantiate this theory.

On a much later occasion my parents, my sister Ba and I were driving to Italy via the Mont Cenis pass. We were aiming for the small town of Orta, situated on a promontory sticking out into Lake Orta. Just before arriving, I edged out in order to overtake a slow lorry; this is always a precarious operation when driving in Europe in a car bought in the UK, because the driver cannot see if there is anything coming in the opposite direction. On this occasion, we collided with a small car travelling in the opposite direction, which landed up in the road-side ditch. No-one was hurt, but the local *carabinieri* turned up, arrested us and drove us off to Orta police station, where we were locked up behind bars. A crowd of local inhabitants assembled outside our gaol, baying for our blood. Things were getting increasingly ugly, when suddenly the tables were turned. One of the colleagues of our group of carabinieri had fallen off his motor bike, and injured himself quite badly. My father saw his chance and shouted *"Sono dottore!"* They immediately let us out of the gaol, my father administered what emergency treatment he could, and we, the lynch mob and the *carabinieri* all ended up in the local *albergo* for a drink together. Nothing further was ever heard of this incident and we proceeded on to Montepulciano, a medieval and Renaissance hill town in southern Tuscany, renowned for its *Vino Nobile*. Montepulciano was, according to legend, founded by The Etruscan king, Lars Porsena of Clusium, immortalised by Lord Macaulay in his epic poem *"Horatio"* inspired by the conflict between Etruria and Rome in about 508 BC, which starts:

"Lars Porsena of Clusium, by the Nine Gods he swore
That the great house of Tarquin should suffer wrong no more.
By the Nine Gods he swore it, and named a trysting day,
And bade his messengers ride forth, East and West and South and North,
To summon his array."

One of the places visited by my parents was Sofia, Bulgaria. Here they were unhappy to find that the only toilet paper provided in their hotel consisted of neatly torn square sheets of "*Pravda*", bound together by a piece of string threaded through a hole in one of the corners, and usually with a picture of Stalin or Lenin on them. My mother couldn't put up with this, so she decided to go to the British Embassy to complain. At the reception desk was a young woman from Lancashire, who took one look at my mother and said "Oh! I bet I know what you want", and produced from under the counter a roll of toilet paper with 'Government Property' stamped on every sheet! This was a rather uncomfortable product to use, being hard – not at all like some celebrated brands of toilet paper, and at the end of this episode my mother was not sure that she wouldn't really have preferred "*Pravda*"!

In the Sixth Form at Clifton, the School's main objective was to get as many pupils as possible into universities, preferably Oxford or Cambridge, and thereby maintaining its position in the league tables, which were published in order to guide parents in their choice of higher educational establishment for their offspring. Eventually I got a Minor Open Scholarship to Trinity College, Cambridge, mainly, I was told, on the basis of a good performance in the mathematics papers. There was an element of luck in this; the night before the scholarship examination, I happened to be revising my coordinate geometry, using a book entitled "*Elementary Coordinate Geometry*", by AS Ramsey. This book gave a number of elegant examples of solutions to problems, and one of these, by chance, was the one I had been looking at on the previous evening. So I simply regurgitated this proof as the answer to one of the questions in the paper. Anyone who has taken a similar examination knows that this sort of event gives a tremendous fillip to one's confidence, and thus buoyed up, I was able to rattle off the solutions to the rest of the problems in the paper. The average medical student hated maths of any sort; even the appearance in a textbook of such a simple relationship as the Henderson-Hasselbach *equation (Eqn. 1) shown at the end of this paragraph (from which one could calculate one of the variables out of the membrane potential and the intra- and extra-cellular concentrations of an ion, such as potassium, to which the cell membrane was permeable) caused the student rapidly to turn to the next page, which was hopefully unsullied by such monstrosities. I have always kept up my mathematics and used it often in my scientific papers.

(The Henderson-Hasselbalch equation, referred to above, describes the relationship between the pH of a solution and the concentrations of a weak acid anion and the undissociated form of the acid:

$$pH = pK_a + \log_{10}\{[A^-]/[HA]\} \quad\ldots\ldots\ldots\ldots\ldots\ldots\ldots\ldots\ldots\ldots\ldots\ldots(1)$$

Here *pH is the negative logarithm (to the base 10) of the hydrogen ion concentration (more strictly, the hydrogen ion activity), pK_a the similar logarithm of the dissociation constant, and the square brackets indicate the concentrations of the anion [A⁻] of the acid and the undissociated acid [HA]. This relationship may be obtained simply by writing down the Law of Mass Action:

$$K_a = ([H^+] \times [A^-])/[HA] \quad\ldots\ldots\ldots\ldots\ldots\ldots\ldots\ldots\ldots\ldots\ldots\ldots(2)$$

and taking logarithms of both sides of the equation.)

References

1) "*Vitai Lampada*", Sir Henry Newbolt, 1897

2) "*Lays of Ancient Rome*", Macaulay TB, 1842

3) In "*A History of Western Philosophy*", Russell B. p.673. George Allen and Unwin, Woking, UK

"*Winterbottom, D.* "Dynasty – The Polack family and the Jewish House at Clifton (1878-2005)".

Chapter 2

University

At Trinity, I lived in Whewell's Court for three years in somewhat inhospitable rooms. There was no form of heating except for a gas ring for boiling a kettle. So I acquired a builder's brick, which I heated on the gas ring, and this raised the temperature a degree or two. Cambridge must be one of the coldest cities in the country, being ravaged by winds from the North Pole, which blow in across the Fens. Whewell's Court was graced by the statue of a naked woman, possibly a mermaid, which was continually desecrated by pigeon droppings. The toilets and bathrooms were downstairs, and were even colder, so I took a bath as infrequently as possible, and, as at Clifton, preferred constipation to visiting the loos. Years later I found out who William Whewell was. He was born in 1794, the son of a carpenter. He won an Exhibition to Trinity, having received some private instruction in mathematics, though he got a prize for his authorship of an epic poem on Boadicea. He graduated as the second Wrangler in 1816 – Wranglers are the accolades given to students who obtain first class degrees in Mathematics at Cambridge, and are ordered according to one's place in the mark list. His friends at Cambridge included John Herschel (1792-1871), later a distinguished astronomer, and Charles Babbage (1791-1871), the co-inventor with Ada, Lady Lovelace, of the idea of the programmable computer. Whewell had wider interests than mathematics, such as writing books or papers on architecture of German churches, astronomy, physics, crystallography, poetry and religion. Many of his friends approached him to suggest names for many of the scientific inventions and discoveries of the day. Thus he produced 'anode', 'cathode' and 'ion' for Michael Faraday, and 'scientist' for the poet Samuel Taylor Coleridge. He also wrote extensively on the philosophy of science, especially on the inductive process. I guess that he foreshadows Karl Popper's *"The Logic of Scientific Discover"*. Returning to Babbage and Lady Lovelace, the latter's name is painted decoratively on the wall just below the ceiling in the foyer of the old Torridon Hotel, in which my wife and I stayed on occasion. Ada (1815-1852) was the only legitimate child of the poet Lord Byron, whose numerous other children were born out of wedlock.

Ada married William, Lord King, in 1835. King owned a number of estates, including his grand shooting lodge on Loch Torridon, which is how Ada's name came to be painted on the wall of the foyer. Byron separated from his wife Anne shortly after Ada's birth, and went off to fight in the Greek War of Independence, in which he died of disease at Missolonghi in western Greece. Ada had obvious mathematical talents, which led to a friendship with another British mathematician, Charles Babbage. The latter had invented a mechanical calculating machine, which he named 'The Analytical Engine'. Ada had translated an article by an Italian mathematician, Luigi Menabrea, which she supplemented with notes of her own, containing, *inter alia*, an algorithm encoded for processing data by machine. These notes are considered to provide the world's first computer programme. It is possible to stay now at Torridon House (though another hotel was built a few years ago at a nearby site, without the inscriptions,) and it was voted the best Scottish hotel in 2013.

To return to Cambridge University, the main court of Trinity was Great Court. This was entered via the Great Gate, opposite the entrance to Whewell's Court. On the outside of the Great Gate, there are a number of heraldic shields, derived from the coats of arms of various founders and early benefactors. The most intriguing of these is painted completely white, and under it is the inscription *"De mortuis infans"*, denoting that the shield belonged to either a stillborn baby or one who had died in early infancy. Over the Great Gate was a set of rooms, the previous home of Isaac Newton and his pet bear. The outside of the Great Gate also had over its arch a statue of the founder, Henry VIII, originally bearing a sceptre, but this had long been replaced, by some irreverent student, with a chair leg! The Great Court itself is of vast dimensions, and the architecture appears to have no set plan. Around the inside of Great Court are a number of staircases, leading to the rooms occupied by either lecturers or students. On the left was a staircase where the Senior Tutor of the day, a Mr. Rattenbury, had his rooms, and to which you were summoned for punishment after being caught at one or other of number of misdemeanours. One of these was being caught by the Proctors after a certain hour in the evening without wearing your academic gown. One of the punishments for such heinous offences was being 'gated', which meant being confined to your rooms after dark for a number of days or weeks. The Great Court of Trinity achieved universal fame in the film *"Chariots of Fire"*, which depicts the history of Eric Liddell and Harold Abrahams, who represented Great Britain at the Olympic Games in Paris in 1924. One of their challenges was to race around the inside of the Great Court whilst the clock on

Trinity College Church struck twelve noon. This was not quite as difficult as it might seem, since a curious agreement had been reached between Trinity and the immediately adjacent St. John's College. The problem was that the noise and general cacophony of the clocks of both Colleges going off together was intolerable, so the solution was reached that the Trinity College clock would strike twice in succession on each hour, once for Trinity and once for St. John's. Thus Liddell and Abrahams had twice the time expected to complete their race. Another feat of these two athletes was said to be that they managed to leap up the whole flight of stairs from the court into the lobby outside the Great Hall in one bound. The Great Hall, where we all ate, had a wooden High Table on a dais under the great Holbein portrait of Henry VIII, and three further lines of wooden tables stretching down the hall, where the students ate. At the beginning of a meal, grace was intoned in Latin by two senior dons, one at each end of the High Table, speaking alternate lines of the lengthy prayer. Around the walls of the Great Hall were portraits of many scientific luminaries who had been Masters or Fellows of the College. These included, *inter alia*, Isaac Newton, JJ Thomson, Ernest Rutherford (who was the first to split the atom, and, therefore, did the early groundwork for the atomic bomb), and Edgar Adrian, who received a Nobel prize for his discovery that the intensity of sensation produced when a sensory nerve fired off was signalled by the frequency of the nerve impulses generated and not by their amplitude. When I was at Trinity, the Master was at first George Macaulay Trevelyan, of *"English Social History"* fame, and later Edgar Adrian, who used to invite the College undergraduates, in batches of ten, to take wine with him in the Master's Lodge, which was situated just to the right of the Great Steps. At these events, Adrian appeared wearing the insignia of the Order of Merit around his neck. I had a number of lectures from Lord Adrian in Part 2 of the Natural Science Tripos (*vide infra*). There were only about twelve of us at these lectures; it was apparent that Adrian had a peculiar hatred of students resting their feet on the dais from which he was addressing us. He used to retreat away from our feet, until he could go back no further because of the presence of the wall of the room. This only made us stick our feet further on to the dais, and Adrian's only escape after he had hit the wall behind him was to terminate the lecture.

Passing through the passage way between the Great Hall and the stairs to the Junior Common Room, one reached Neville's Court, an austere, elegant space, and south of this were the 'Backs', referring to the area around the River Cam. There were several places where one could hire a punt to propel yourself up and down the river. A favourite student occupation was to stand on one of the several bridges over the river and snatch the pole from some unwary punter as he (or she) passed under the bridge. This usually resulted in the punter falling into the river, and usually his girlfriend too! There were certain parts of the river where the bottom was very muddy; your punt pole tended to stick in this mud, with similar consequences to the pole-snatching alluded to above! At Cambridge, the punter operates from the raised deck at one end of the punt, in contrast to those cowardly creatures at Oxford who stand at the other end of the punt, when travelling down the Isis (the name given to the Thames as it passes through the city). A favourite punting trip at Cambridge was to go up the river to the small village of Grantchester, immortalised by World War I poet Rupert Brooke (1887-1915), in *"The Old Vicarage, Grantchester"*:

"say, is there Beauty yet to find?
And Certainty? And Quiet kind?
Deep meadows yet, for to forget
The lies, and truths, and pain? …oh? Yet
Stands the Church clock at ten to three?
And is there honey still for tea?"

Rupert Brooke died in 1915 from an infected mosquito bite, inflicted whilst sailing to Gallipoli as part of the British Mediterranean Expeditionary Force. I can assure readers that the last time I was in Grantchester, the church clock still stood at ten to three, no doubt at the insistence of the parish councillors, who had recognised this feature as a profitable tourist attraction.

One of the annual events at Cambridge was the singing of madrigals by the choir of King's College Chapel (one of the great masterpieces of English Perpendicular architecture) from punts under King's Bridge. The madrigals in my time were conducted by the celebrated Boris Ord, the choirmaster of King's Chapel Choir. This madrigal session always concluded with *"Draw on, Sweet Night"* by John Wilbye, as the choir slowly drifted down the river in the gloaming, bearing candles to light their way. The only downside of this romantic and nostalgic event was that the backs were also inhabited by herds of cattle, and in the dusk one frequently accidentally sat down in a cow pad, necessitating instant ablutions! Another event at Cambridge which I vividly remember was a concert given by Kathleen Ferrier (1912-1953), the contralto, accompanied, as usual, by Gerald Moore, on the piano. She was particularly great at English folk songs, such as *"O! waly, waly!"* and *"Down by the Sally Gardens"* She died in her early forties, of cancer of the breast; during a performance of Gluck's *"Orfeo ed Euridice"* at the Royal Opera House, Covent Garden, her left femur fractured, due to a secondary tumour. However, she insisted on singing her remaining arias and took her curtain calls, discreetly supported by other members of the cast, before being admitted to University College Hospital, where she later passed away. I have a much prized recording of her folk songs, and of her arias from *"Orfeo"*.

To return to the more academic side of life at Cambridge, at that time in the 1950s one initially worked for Part 1 of the Natural Sciences Tripos, which included anatomy, physiology and some biochemistry. In anatomy, the first task was to dissect the human body. The term 'Tripos' is derived from the three-legged stool on which students used to sit in olden times to face their examiners. The cadavers came either from people who willed their bodies after death to be used for 'medical research', or from vagrants who had no known relatives to bury them. In earlier times, bodies for dissection were less easy to get hold of. Thus, the celebrated pair of Burke and Hare carried out a series of murders in 1827 and 1828 and sold the bodies to medical schools. Their favoured technique was to get the prospective victim drunk and then smother him (or her). Hare was granted immunity from prosecution in return for testifying against Burke. The latter was hung in January 1929, in front of a crowd exceeding 20,000, and was publicly dissected in the anatomy theatre of the University of Edinburgh. The crowd, however, took a dim view of Hare, despite his being granted immunity, and pursued him diligently. It is said that he was caught and thrown into a lime pit, which caused him to be blinded, and he ended his days as a blind beggar on the streets of London, though this tale was never confirmed.

Every student of anatomy was paired with another, who read out the instructions from Cunningham's manual of dissection, whilst the other did the cutting. The first part of the body I had to dissect was the leg. As we got to the groin region, it was apparent that our cadaver was not displaying the features described in the manual. It turned out that the cadaver had an unhealed fracture of the neck or the femur, and that walking on this leg had distorted the anatomy. At the end of dissection of each section of the body (i.e. head and neck, thorax, abdomen, arm and leg), you received a *viva voce* examination from one of the demonstrators. Unless you passed, you were not allowed to go on to the next section. The Professor of Anatomy of the time – in my case, JD Boyd – appeared in the dissection room from time to time to make sure that everything was proceeding *à la mode*. At the end of the series, a technician came along and sawed off the skull cap, so that you could examine the meninges and the foramina at the base of the skull. The cadavers for dissection had been injected with some red substance to show up some of the blood vessels and then preserved in formalin. One's copy of Cunningham's dissection manual became impregnated with formalin and stank to high heaven forever thereafter. The medical students' bible and reference book in anatomy was *"Gray's Anatomy"*, a weighty tome of over 1500 pages. I did not have to buy a copy, since one was passed down to me by my cousin, Bernard Peck, who had trained at Bart's Hospital Medical School. This is only possible for anatomy texts, amongst all the books used by medical students, since in the case of physiology and biochemistry and medicine, new discoveries are continually being made, and a text book in these subjects rapidly gets out of date. It is not too easy to make a new discovery in the field of gross human anatomy. Human evolution is not proceeding that fast! During my time as a student at Cambridge, new anatomy textbooks by Hamilton, Boyd and Mossman appeared which was much smaller and more user-friendly. Today, medical students, quite sensibly, are not required to learn all the anatomical *minutiae* that we had to clutter our brains with. They are provided with already prepared specimens, dissected in a way which ensures that the features which medical students really do have to know about are easily seen.

Physiology

The Physiology Department at Cambridge had a star-studded cast during my time, including Edgar Adrian, Alan Hodgkin and Andrew Huxley. I have said something about these Nobel Laureates above, but they were not the best lecturers in the world; many students found that they could best pass their examinations by listening to a Mr. Tunnicliffe, who hadn't done any research of note, but certainly had the gift of putting the subject over. The biochemists at Cambridge were equally distinguished, one of the best known being David Keilin (1887-1963), an entomologist and parasitologist, who initiated the discovery of the cytochromes. Cytochromes are proteins containing haem and they form major links in the electron transfer chain, which remove electrons from substrates and transfer them ultimately to oxygen, thus mediating a large number of biological oxidations. This work was done on the horse parasite *Gastrophilus intestinalis*, which explains why someone who was by training a career parasitologist and entomologist was responsible for this fundamental discovery. This is, of course, not the only way in which work on horses has contributed to physiological knowledge. In 1714, Stephen Hales (1677-1761), an ordained priest, inserted a brass tube into the carotid artery of a horse and measured the height to which the blood rose. This was the first attempt to measure blood pressure, and resulted in the death of the horse. Hales also took wax casts of the ventricles of the heart, to measure their volumes. From this and the pulse rate, he was able to make one of the first measurements of cardiac output. He also described the function of the mitral and aortic valves of the heart during the phases of the cardiac cycle. Furthermore, he developed a double lumen bladder catheter, and, using this, attempted to dissolve bladder stones. He also prophetically suggested that electricity played a role in nerve conduction.

It was of obvious importance for medical students to gain knowledge of human nutrition. The department at Cambridge which instructed us on this subject was located in an annex of the Biochemistry building in the Downing Street campus, and was led by Robert A. McCance and Elsie Widdowson, who produced the standard work on the composition of foodstuffs, e.g. protein, carbohydrate, fat, vitamins and minerals. McCance was an extremely thin man, whereas the Elsie Widdowson was, shall we say, rather the opposite! McCance cycled to work each day, tying up his trouser legs with string, rather than use cycle clips; the string remaining all day while he was at work. He only had one meal a day, and this was enormous, reputedly containing 6-7,000 calories, despite his thinness. This is the sort of feature that is seen in thyrotoxicosis (over-activity of the thyroid gland), but it was obvious that McCance did not suffer from this condition. One of their Lecturers was Dr. Romain Hervey, who battled with the question of whether, when cast adrift in a lifeboat at sea, you should, or should not, drink sea water. According to the French expert on this subject, Alain Bombard (1924 -2005), one could survive crossing the Atlantic in a small boat without provisions by eating fish as a source of both freshwater and food, together with a limited amount of seawater. There was a later (unsubstantiated) claim that Bombard had secretly taken a supply of fresh water with him.

As in most universities, the means of transport from one's college to the lecture halls (in Downing Street) for medical students, was either on foot or by bicycle. The whole of Cambridge was littered with bikes and bike stands, and it was important to have some sort of wheel lock, since a certain amount of unauthorised 'borrowing' was common. For tourists driving around the city, cyclists were an absolute menace, since they clearly believed that they had precedence over all other traffic!

At Cambridge, you could choose to do Part 1 of the Natural Sciences Tripos in either two or three years. Passing with a degree of Third Class or above was sufficient to get awarded the BA (Cantab) degree. Those who were on the brighter side tended to do Part 1 in two years and used the third year for a Part 2. I chose to do my Part 2 in Physiology. The examination at the end of Part 2 consisted of a single paper containing three questions, and you had a choice of attempting one, two or three questions. If you really knew your stuff you only answered one question, spending the whole three hours on this single question, thus demonstrating your depth of knowledge, so I spent the whole three hours on a question on nerve conduction, simply regurgitating what I had swotted up. This was enough to do the trick, and I got a First Class degree.

My tutor at Cambridge was William Rushton, a Fellow of the Royal Society, a good mathematician, and a competent player of the bassoon. Although in his earlier years he had worked with Alan Hodgkin on nerve conduction, he later shifted to visual physiology. He used me as a subject in one of his experiments, and my reward was to join him in the paper in *"Nature"* which followed. The main conclusion was that the main factor in dark adaptation is an increase in the quantum sensitivity of the retina[1].

With this behind me I found it was relatively easy to get into The London Hospital Medical College to do my clinical training. At the interview I was confronted by a panel which contained John Ellis, the great UK guru on Medical Education, and Sub-Dean of the London at the time. During the interview, I was asked by one of the other members of the panel whether I knew anything about a village near Plymouth (which the panel members knew was my home town from the paperwork in from of them). I said that it was the birthplace of the artist Sir Joshua Reynolds, but, apart from that, I was not aware of it having any other claim to distinction. There was a tremendous guffaw from the panel members, one of whom said "Are you not also aware that was also the birthplace of the Dean?" I thought that I had blown my chances of admission, but fortunately, the other members of the panel were so amused by this *faux pas* that they let me in.

The Medical College boasted a substantial museum of 'pots', which contained preserved specimens obtained at operation or autopsy, and was used as a learning centre for students during their pathology attachment. It was well-known for containing part of the skeleton of Joseph Merrick, who suffered from a condition known as 'leontiasis ossei' which hideously deforms the bones, creating a very ugly appearance, and he was known as 'The Elephant Man'. Merrick used to wear a mask over his head with two holes cut for him to see through, and this is also in the museum. Merrick was befriended by a surgeon at the hospital, Sir Frederick Treves, who wrote a book entitled *"The Elephant Man and other Reminiscences"*. Treves was one of the Honorary Sergeant Surgeons to King Edward VII; two days before his coronation, the King developed what is now known as appendicitis, and Treves recommended draining the infected organ through a small abdominal incision – an operation which carried a high mortality rate, so the King at first refused to allow it. Treves pointed out that, if he did not have it done, he would be attending his funeral rather than his coronation, so the King eventually agreed. The next day he was sitting up in bed, smoking a cigar. The museum had one another purpose; the final medical examinations had a Pathology practical section, in which the terrified candidates were shown a series of pots, and asked to make diagnoses of the diseases from which the patients from whom these specimens were obtained were suffering.

One day at a lecture in the Bearsted Theatre, I perceived in the audience a girl whom I had not previously noticed. I turned to the student sitting next to me and asked who she was. He replied "That's Barbara Boucher" (Plate 2). This was a somewhat significant piece of information, for she was to be my future wife!

Undergraduate medical education at The London Hospital Medical College followed the pretty standard pattern adopted by UK medical schools, i.e. two years of preclinical studies, followed by three years of clinical work in the wards, and pathology and pharmacology, together with a number of lectures every week. In this we were better off than many continental medical schools, which provided an intensive course of lectures but virtually no contact with patients until after qualification. The problem was that UK medical students often got very bored during the preclinical course, not being able to see the relevance of what they were being taught to the clinical course to follow, or, indeed to their clinical careers to follow. At Western Reserve Medical School in Cleveland, Ohio, they had introduced a more innovative system, in which patients were introduced from the very beginning of the course. Thus, for example, when the students were learning about the anatomy, physiology and biochemistry of bone, they were introduced to patients with fractures, or with rickets. This was known as 'integration'. Our Dean, John Ellis, had a very good relationship with Thomas Hale Ham, at Western Reserve, who had introduced an integrated programme at that School. 'Integration' implies that at the same time as you are learning the basic medical sciences, you are also doing clinical attachments so that you can see the relevance of the basic medical sciences to what follows.

The clinical course at The London when I was a student consisted of two periods, each of two months, attached to a medical firm and similar periods on the surgical wards. There were then several weeks of morbid anatomy, bacteriology and pharmacology. The whole thing culminated in the final examinations, supervised by the Universities of Oxford, Cambridge or London, according to where you had done your preclinical course. These were terrifying ordeals, and certain examiners gained the reputation of failing as many students as possible. The course at The London always had a period of two months (the so-called 'elective') during the Clinical Course, in which the student could choose whatever he or she wanted to do, provided it had some relevance to Medicine. This is why John Ellis suggested that two of my fellow students, David Hughes and Peter Richardson, and myself, should spend our elective seeing how things were done in American medical schools. David and I went to Western Reserve, and Peter to Charlottesville, Virginia, which had a rather more conventional course than did Western Reserve. Our experiences were recounted in a paper[3] in the "*Lancet*" entitled '*Medical Students Look West*'. During our stay in the USA we also visited some other medical schools which had innovatory programmes of one sort or another. Thus Boston University and Tufts Medical College had home-care programmes; American law allowed students in their final years the opportunity to visit patients in their homes in the slums of Boston and prescribe from a limited list of drugs. Though this did not provide the standard of care that attention from qualified doctors would give, it was usually better than nothing. One of the relaxations we had at Western Reserve was to join the students at beach parties at night on the shores of Lake Erie. Although we ate and drank a good deal at these affairs, no swimming was advisable. This was because a few hundred yards along the shore was the mouth of the Cuyahoga River, which contained so much of the effluent from the industrial parts of Cleveland that it frequently caught fire spontaneously! Another hazard at Cleveland was self-engendered. David used to wander around the streets wearing his Cheltenham College blazer. This was a black confection with vertical red stripes, and the local youths followed him around in wonderment, never having seen anything like this before and obviously thinking that this was a creature from outer space!

David and I took the opportunity of visiting Peter Richardson in Charlottesville. There, in the Deep South, life proceeded and a much slower pace than up north in Cleveland. There was a sort of sultry relaxation pervading the whole atmosphere, and this was reflected in the agonising slowness of the southern drawl. Thus the simple greeting "How are you?" came out as "How are yaaaaaaaaarl today?" over about thirty seconds. At night, one basked in the syrupy atmosphere, watching the fireflies. Some fourteen years later I visited the Western Reserve campus again and was asked if I had noticed anything different since my previous visit. On replying in the negative, my hosts told me that the Medical School had found it necessary to provide room for a substantial new building. So they had simply dug under the Babies' and Childrens' Hospital, inserted rollers under it, and dragged the whole building aside using gigantic tractors. Apparently the Americans, who are clearly capable of anything, were quite used to this sort of thing! During our visit we had the opportunity of visiting Niagara and took a boat which sailed right up to the bottom of the Falls, where you had to have almost total coverage with waterproof clothes because of the tremendous amount of spray.

Our journey home after our visit was on a tramp steamer operating out of the Hudson River. This was a pretty gruelling experience; although the cost of the passage was very low, there were indeed serious drawbacks. There was thick fog all the way back and the ship's foghorn sounded off every three minutes, meaning that we got no sleep at all, since our apology for a cabin was located immediately under the foghorn. Secondly, the ship's Chief Engineer insisted that we played bridge with him every night; since none of us really knew how to play this game, we lost considerable sums of money. The ship docked at Swansea after ten days of this sort of torture, in the commercial part of the dock, and we had to drag our luggage under the trucks of the goods trains waiting to move off. Eventually, we managed to find the customs office, and after hours of waiting, were let through. I proceeded to the railway station and asked the girl at the ticket office for a ticket to Plymouth. "Where is it you want to go?" she said. I repeated "Plymouth", but still she did not understand. I eventually had to write it down for her. She took one look at the bit of paper, and said in her sing-song Welsh accent "Oh, it's Ply-mouth you mean. Why didn't you say so in the first place?" Wales is truly a foreign country!

I must pause here to describe another, literally nauseating, journey I made to America on the liner MV *Britannic*. We departed from Liverpool and all was serene till we made a stop at Cork in Southern Ireland, where we picked up two hundred nuns. I have no idea why they were going to America – whether they were going for charitable purposes, or just to spread the Gospel. Be that as it may, we ran into some extremely rough weather; every few minutes the propellers came out of the water with a tremendous whirring noise. The nuns simply lined up on the deck, vomiting over the side, whilst counting their rosaries and praying for salvation. Some of them simply couldn't quite make it, and the stairs from the lower deck were covered in pools of vomit. I have never been subject to sea-sickness, but managed to slip in some nun's stomach contents deposited on the stairs, an accident which caused considerable bruising!

Meanwhile, Barbara had developed somewhat of a reputation in Forensic Medicine because of her discovery, as a student, of the features of the foetal and neonatal pelvis which helped one to distinguish the sex of the foetus or neonate. To be able to do this was an important advance in criminology and forensic medicine. She had produced a simple instrument for this purpose, and this led to an invitation by a well-known physical anthropologist (Mildred Trotter, of the University of St. Louis, Missouri) to examine the bodies of babies of negro origin to see if the same methods could be applied. On her arrival, she was confronted with the corpses of about 400 dead babies stored in a deep-freeze. She dissected out the pelves and then boiled them to remove residual flesh, in order to be able to get at the bones. Fortunately, she returned in a comparatively sane state from these macabre activities!

Barbara had been sent by her parents to a couple of rather *avant-garde* schools, Kilquhanity House and Beltane. She was summarily removed from the first of these, because her father dropped in unexpectedly one day, and found her cooking a 'fry-up' on an upturned electric fire in a hay loft – the dangers of conflagration were obviously extreme. One of her school friends at Beltane was Luke Gertler, the son of the well-known painter, Mark Gertler (1891-1939). Possibly the best known of Mark's works is "*The Merry-Go-Round*", which to many is a cynical commentary on life in general; it is now exhibited in the Tate Gallery. We once visited Luke in his home – he has a substantial collection of his father's works.

A feature of the US medical education system was that the US student was always made to feel part of the clinical team, and not treated with mere tolerance, as in the UK. In that way a sense of responsibility was instilled, which enhanced the educational experience. The average UK medical student was fairly terrified by the eminent consultant whose ward rounds they were graciously allowed to attend. I remember being on the firm of Sir Horace Evans (later Lord Evans), who was one of the Queen's physicians. He had a reputation of being an excellent diagnostician. He only did one ward round per week, the rest of his time being taken up by his extensive private practice in Harley Street. It was the job of his Senior Registrar to meet him on these occasions in the foyer of the hospital after alighting from his chauffeur-driven Rolls Royce, which had conveyed him from his private practice in Harley Street to the slums of the East End, and to conduct him to a patient whose diagnosis had eluded everyone else. On one occasion he was taken to see a girl aged about twenty, with an apparently undiagnosable fever (known as a 'PUO'- pyrexia of unknown origin). The maestro adjusted his shirt cuffs to precisely one third of an inch below the jacket cuffs of his Saville Row suit, put a hairy paw into the girl's axilla and then looked at her temperature chart. He then declared

"She has glands, she has fever – glandular fever!"

The Senior Registrar then thrust a piece of paper in front of him, saying "But, Sir – look at the blood count!"

The maestro swept it aside, declaring

"We only need the blood count in difficult cases!

On another occasion, he invited me to look at the back of a patient's eye, using an *ophthalmoscope.

"Well", he said, "what's the diagnosis?"

I, having seen a very pale optic disc, said nervously "Optic atrophy, Sir!"

By good fortune, this happened to be correct, and the Great Man patted my on the head, saying "Ha! A budding neurologist, I see!" This episode put me off neurology for good, which was a little unfortunate, since my clinical tutor, James Nathaniel Blau, was an excellent neurologist. In those days, the emphasis in Neurology was in diagnosis and prognosis, since there was not much one could do in the way of treatment.

This brings me to another curious incident. One day I met Nat Blau for my weekly tutorial session. Nat Blau was a man of short stature – 5ft. 4 inchs, perhaps, whereas I was over 6ft tall. He looked up at me, saying

"Cohen, have you ever seen a patient with DTs (i.e. *delirium tremens*)?"
"No", said I, peering down at him.
"Well" said Nat, "come along to my ward and I will show you how to deal with such a patient!"

So we proceeded to the neurological ward, where there was an enormous red-headed Irishman hiding in terror under the bedclothes, because of the green spiders and other noxious creatures that he could see climbing up the windows opposite him. Nat thought for a moment or two, put his black bag on the end of the bed, took out an ophthalmoscope, switched it on and advanced upon the Irishman. The latter put out a brawny air and swept Nat and his instrument to the other side of the ward, shouting

"Take that bloody flamethrower away!"

I concluded that Nat, who was a relatively new appointment, hadn't any previous experience of patients with DTs either! There was in fact a lot of drunkenness in the East End of London, which is of course near the docks, and the area is thus full of seamen letting their hair down after long weeks on the oceans. There was, however, a group of local drunkards frequently admitted to The London with DTs; they got to know that young doctors and medical students were fascinated by their hallucinations and clearly tried to amuse them. I remember one sufferer claiming that he could see 'yellow lorries driven by skeletons'!

One of the patients shown to me by Nat Blau had the condition known as myasthenia gravis. This is an auto-immune disease, in which the body makes antibodies to sites on the plasma membranes of skeletal muscle fibres (known as motor end plates). The consequence is that that the neurotransmitter substance, acetylcholine, which is released by motor nerve endings, cannot stimulate contraction of the muscle. The symptoms develop over weeks or months, often starting with ptosis (drooping of the eyelids) and diplopia (double vision), and gradually spreading to the rest of the skeletal musculature. Eventually the muscles of respiration are involved, and, if the diagnosis is not made and appropriate treatment not given, death can ensue. Medical treatment consists of the administration of anticholinesterase drugs, such as neostigmine, which prevent the destruction of the neurotransmitter – but this approach is not curative, and patients may become resistant to it. However, an American surgeon, Alfred Blalock, (1899-1964), had shown that removal of a tumour of the *thymus gland in a patient with myasthenia gravis produced a much more sustained improvement, and correctly predicted that removal of the whole thymus gland would be of value in patients who had myasthenia gravis, but no thymus tumour. The operation was taken up in the UK by Geoffrey Keynes[2] (1887-1982) at Bart's. He was a member of a small group of Cambridge families who excelled in several fields and tended to marry people from these families. Thus Geoffrey Keynes' elder brother was the well-known economist, John Maynard Keynes. I have already referred to Edgar Adrian, sometime Master of Trinity College; his daughter married the physiologist Richard Keynes, who was the great-grandson of Charles Darwin. He showed that the nerve impulse is accompanied by a movement of sodium ions into the nerve fibre and an exit of potassium ions; and lastly (and leastly (!)) taught me when I was at Cambridge! This galaxy of talent included both Fellows of the Royal Society and Nobel Laureates! Though it is highly unfashionable to mention the subject since the efforts of the Nazis in World War II, this family history suggests that there is something to be said for eugenics! A good deal of the flavour of the atmosphere created by these families can be obtained by reading "*Period Piece*", a memoir by Gwen Raverat (1885-1957) which has many anecdotes about the Darwins.

One of my hobbies at The London was sailing with the United Hospitals Sailing Club, which was based at Burnham-on-Crouch in Essex. This was set up by The Medical Schools in London. The club owned its own sailing dinghies and there was a strict practical test of one's ability to perform such manoeuvres as tacking, running, gybing, and keeping the boat reasonably upright in a strong wind, before being allowed to take a dinghy out on one's own. Shortly after passing my test, I took a boat out at night – this turned out to be a rather disastrous adventure. Firstly, the River Crouch has muddy banks, and the river itself is rather muddy, too. So it became extremely difficult to distinguish bank from river, and I kept on going aground on the shore. This often meant getting out of the boat to push it off, getting very wet in the process. Secondly, I inadvertently sailed across the mooring rope of some rather opulent looking cruiser. My centre plate caught on the rope, and I found myself dragging the cruiser behind me – it seemed as if I were towing the liner the *Queen Mary*, since objects at night tend to look larger than they actually are! Before long, the irate owner of the cruiser appeared on deck in his pyjamas and yelled

"Can't sail, can't steer, and can't do any bloody thing".

I had the presence of mind to pull up the centre plate and the cruiser and its apoplectic owner vanished into the night as I raced away from the scene!

One day, on the way back from a day's sailing I suddenly coughed up a lot of blood. This turned out to be due to tuberculosis (TB) in the apex of my right lung. I was admitted to the London under the care of Dr. Lloyd Rusby, the senior chest physician at the London. I think I had probably acquired TB from a patient I clerked with *systemic lupus erythematosus, who had been treated with massive doses of steroids (these drugs greatly increase the susceptibility to TB, because of their immuno-suppressive effect). The patient subsequently died, and at autopsy proved to have military tuberculosis, a form of TB which affects many organs of the body simultaneously. In fact, her lungs were almost a pure culture of *Mycobacterium tuberculosis*. Fortunately, by this time there were effective drugs against TB, although this entailed having painful injections of streptomycin injected into my buttocks, several times a week. The administration of streptomycin alone rapidly results in resistance to the drug, so I also had to take para-aminosalicylic acid (which caused one's underpants to become stained orange), and isoniazid, which, fortunately, had a somewhat euphoriant effect. At that time, the practice was, in addition to the drugs, to excise the lesion surgically, and so two segments of the upper lobe of my right lung were duly removed by Sir Geoffrey Todd, of the King Edward VII Sanatorium near Midhurst in West Sussex. Sir Geoffrey was a keen cricketer in the grounds of the sanatorium and used to demonstrate his skills against local teams on the pitch in front of the sanatorium. He demanded that all patients who were not confined to bed came out to watch him and his team perform. No one excises such tuberculous lesions these days, since it is recognised that an adequate course of the drugs is all that is needed. Though this operation turned out to be quite unnecessary, I have never suffered any obvious difficulty from the loss of a piece of my lung. The only slight problem was that during the operation the stellate ganglion of the sympathetic chain above the apex of my right lung was damaged, causing Horner's syndrome to develop. Horner's syndrome is a combination of ptosis (drooping of the eyelid), meiosis (constriction of the pupil), enophthalmos (sinking in of the eyeball) and decreased sweating of the side of the face. None of this has caused me any significant disability. I had a minor relapse about three years later, but, fortunately, sanatoria had gone out of fashion by then (the Midhurst sanatorium has since been turned into a housing estate), and I took my medication at home. I suspect that Barbara rather enjoyed stabbing my backside with the streptomycin injections thrice weekly! Carting syringes and needles around in the car was a bit of a nuisance. I remember, on one occasion, putting all this equipment on the roof of our car whilst loading the boot with other baggage. We drove off without remembering what was on the roof. Consequently it wasn't long before the syringes, needles and drugs were scattered over the road! No doubt our neighbours rushed off to telephone the police, believing that they had uncovered some sort of drug ring!

Whilst confined to the Midhurst sanatorium, patients were given various forms of occupational therapy to while away the time. This is how I learnt from a local artist (Adrian Hill who was employed to provide occupational therapy for the patients), to paint in watercolours and I have enjoyed this hobby ever since. About one in ten of my efforts has been worth framing. I have tried a few oils, but the only creditable one is shown in Plate 3 which shows Barbara holding two umbrellas, one black and the other pink, in a square in Bruges on a rainy day. The reason why she is holding two umbrellas is not because of the rain and wind, but simply that she had to hold mine whilst I was wielding the camera. Painting outdoors is theoretically the best way to do landscapes, but, once I am at it, it always seems to start to rain, thereby ruining my efforts before I have time to get indoors or erect a large umbrella. I have, therefore, often painted from photographs, which, however, never seem to reproduce the exact colours of the landscape.

My wife and I have also bought quite a large number of watercolours, and gouaches, and a few oils as well. Most of the watercolours have been obtained from Chris Beetles, of Ryder Street, just south of Piccadilly, or from Jeremy Green, lately of the Canon Gallery at Petworth. Chris Beetles used to be a general practitioner in North London, but found that art dealing was more interesting (and, I guess, more profitable). We have a special interest in Victorian watercolours, and have bought works by Albert Goodwin, Cecil Hunt, Hercules Brabazon Brabazon, JMW Turner (prints only!), George Fripp, and William Purser amongst others. Our most prized possession is an oil by Thomas Luny (1759-1837; Plate 4) of old rotting hulks on the shore at his home town, Teignmouth, in Devon, Luny had severe rheumatoid arthritis and this meant that he could only wield a paintbrush with difficulty, but this did not seem to affect the quality of his work. Luny always signed his work on a piece of driftwood which he included in the painting. The former Professor of Physiology at the London, WR ('Bill') Keatinge and his wife, Annette, had a large painting in their dining room in their house in Putney. We thought that this was by Luny, both because of the subject, and the fact that it was signed on a piece of driftwood in the bottom left-hand corner. They were amazed by our apparently profound knowledge of art and confirmed that we were right. Keatinge had a special interest in Environmental Medicine, and was always rushing off to strange places to gather material for his work – one of these places, if my memory serves me correctly, was Krasnoyarsk, in Siberia. He showed that a good deal of heat was lost from the top of the head in cold climates, and insisted that explorers and members of His Majesty's Armed Forces wore woolly hats in these circumstances. This advice is also useful to prevent the development of hypothermia in the elderly. Keatinge's team also tackled the problem of whether, when cast adrift after shipwreck on the high seas, one should drink seawater or suffer severe thirst until it rained (*vide supra* – Alain Bombard). Another pioneer at the London was an anaesthetist, Edgar Pask, who was interested in the design of life *jackets*. The important point was that the life jacket should hold its wearer face up in the water, even when unconscious; so he had himself anaesthetised and thrown into the College swimming pool to test the various designs of jacket and find out which type would float pilots, who had been forced to parachute into the English Channel during World War II, in such a position that their noses were out of the water.

A more recent painting that we have acquired was done by an old school friend of Barbara's, Rosa Branson. She currently specialises in enormous canvasses to decorate town halls and other public rooms. However, we have two of her smaller efforts, both of the still-life variety. Rosa collects objects and paints them arranged in several different ways; thus, one series has a brown jug and a gravy boat and another features a blue jug and a candlestick.

The clinical training at The London included a period in obstetrics and gynaecology. The regulations stipulated that each student should attend a prescribed number of deliveries, before being "signed up". Part of this training was attendance at deliveries in the patient's home. For this experience I was paired with a student, Claude Couve de Murville, who was the scion of a French aristocratic family. When the word came that a patient was about to deliver at home, we rushed to our bicycles, and, accompanied by our chief District Midwife, generally known as 'Gladys', sped along the darkened streets of Whitechapel, often through the previous haunts of Jack the Ripper, to the house of the patient in question, often in the small hours of the morning (birth waits for no-one!). The job of one of the students was to administer an ether anaesthetic, whilst the other assisted Gladys at the other end of the patient. Ether, a highly inflammable and volatile substance, is heavier than air and its fumes therefore tend to spread along the floor. Since the bedroom usually had a blazing open coal or log fire, the risk of the whole lot of us going up in flames was considerable. The women we attended had often had several previous children and had run out of favourite names, so it was their custom to ask the first name of the student who had delivered her. Claude was at the business end on this occasion, but when he answered with his own name her eyes glazed over, so the child got named 'Robert' after myself, as I was administering the anaesthetic.

One of the Consultant Obstetricians at the time was Alan Brews, who, because of his stocky bulldog-like appearance was nicknamed 'Bonzo'. He gave an entertaining lecture entitled 'Foreign Bodies in the Vagina', illustrated by his remarkable collection of the objects he had come across in that situation, the most spectacular of which was a bust of Nelson! Emma Hamilton would have turned in her grave! His consultant colleague was Robert Percival, who was a noted cricketer. On one occasion whilst fielding he rushed to catch a skied ball, not noticing that a staff member of the Department of Anatomy was doing precisely the same thing. There was a clash of heads and both were knocked unconscious! Fortunately, both came round fairly rapidly.

References

1) Rushton WAH and Cohen RD. Visual purple and the course of dark adaptation. *Nature,* 173, 301-304, 1954

2) Cohen RD., Hughes DTD and Richardson PC. Medical Students Look West – impressions of some American medical schools. *Lancet,* August 1957, 407-409

3) Keynes, Geoffrey. *The Gates of Memory.* Clarendon Press, Oxford, 1981. pp. 428

Chapter 3

My career in Medicine

I qualified in Medicine about nine months later than the rest of my class, because of the interruption in training caused by the TB episode. Those who had done their preclinical studies at Cambridge went back to their *alma mater* for the final examination, but since I was obviously anxious to get qualified as soon as possible, I decided to enter the examinations for the Licentiateship of the Royal College of Physicians (LRCP) and Membership of The Royal College of Surgeons (MRCS), which were held more frequently than the Cambridge examination. I particularly remember the MRCS examination, which, needless to say, was somewhat more barbaric than the LRCP. After all the candidates had been assessed, they were left hanging around in a crowd in the foyer of the RCS, awaiting the result. The bedell of the College called each candidate in turn to the foot of the stairs and whispered his result into his or her ear. The successful candidates were directed upstairs where they shook hands with the President and officers of the College and were given some alcoholic refreshment. Those who had failed were directed, in sight of all their peers, to a passageway beside the staircase, which led to the back door, through which they passed unnoticed.

During most of Barbara's and my careers at The London we lived in Beckenham, a suburb in the south east of the metropolis. We had been introduced to Dr. and Mrs K. Ampikaipakan (Ampi) and his wife, Damindi, by Dr. V. Rudralingam, a relative of Ampi's, over the back wall of our garden. They had come over to the UK so that Ampi could prepare for the examination for the Membership of the Royal College of Physicians examination and had rented a house in the adjacent avenue. We were asked if we could introduce him to some patients at The London so that he could hone his clinical and diagnostic skills. Their daughter, Sundari, was at school in a branch of the Girl's Public Day School Trust in Crystal Palace, which our daughter had also attended. This eventually led to their inviting us to their home in Malaysia, to which we have now been to many times. Their house is in Damansara Heights, one of the more upbeat districts of Kuala Lumpur, and has recently been totally re-organised in four storeys, the ground floor being used for cooking, leisure and guest bedrooms, the lower floors being Ampi's and Dandy's domain, the next belonging to Sundari and the top level to their son, Ganesh, who is a writer and columnist working for the *New Straits Times*. Ampi had noted that there was very little expertise on *sarcoidosis in Malaysia, and because of his interest in this condition as it affects the lungs, decided to make another visit to the UK to see Donald Mitchell, Consultant Physician at The Brompton and University College Hospitals, who was the UK expert on this condition.

Kuala Lumpur is not generally regarded as a prime tourist attraction, but this is quite wrong. It contains some quite outstandingly original buildings, some designed by the well-known architect Hijjas Kastouri and his daughter Serena. Kuala Lumpur also has a central market, which contains a large variety of stalls offering an extraordinary range of goods. There are many hangovers from the British colonial era, including the Selangor Cricket Club, the Carcosa, the erstwhile residence of the British Governor, and the Prime Minister's wife's orchid garden. All of these buildings are now used by the Malaysian Government. There is a hierarchical aristocracy, each state having a king, and from these is elected an overall sovereign, who is known as the Yang di Pertuan Agong. At the time of our first visit, the Agong had his palace at Terengganu on the east coast, in the middle of his golf course! Each of the former federated states distributes the title of Dato (female 'Datin'), roughly equivalent to a knighthood, to its more distinguished residents. If a Dato has so distinguished himself in more than one state he is known as Dato Dato (Dato^2 for short), or Dato Dato Dato (Dato^3) if he has this honour in two or three states respectively; the wife of a Dato is given the title 'Datin'. The next grade up in the hierarchy of Malaysian honours is the 'Tansri'; unlike Dato, this is a national honour, and in due course Ampi was made a Tansri. The common Malaysian language, Bahasa Malay, does not have a simple way of writing the plural, such as by adding an 's' to the end of a word. Thus, on Malaysian Airlines (MAS) the stewardess, when making an announcement precedes her remarks by saying Tuan Tuan and Perempuan Perempuan, the equivalent of 'Ladies and Gentlemen' except that the gentlemen precede the ladies in this appellation. Malaysian food is quite interesting, though the Tamil members (e.g. Ampi and Dandy) of the community are usually vegetarians. This, however, did not prevent their general factotum, Nya, cooking some excellent meat dishes for us, usually containing lamb or chicken. Though there are many excellent restaurants in Kuala Lumpur, some of the tastiest food is sold by street vendors and is known as 'hawker food'. Malaysia has some excellent fruits that are not usually obtainable in much of the UK, e.g. rambutans, mangosteens, jack fruit and durians. Rambutans are the most innocuous, but mangosteen juice stains one's skin and clothes red, and the staining is very difficult to remove. Durians have a horrible stench, and it is only with the greatest of difficulty that you can bear to put it in your mouth, but, when it finally gets there, it is delicious. I remember getting stuck behind a lorry containing an enormous load of durians. The stink was so unbearable that we had to stop for a meal somewhere to let it get well ahead of us. Durians grow on enormously tall trees, which you musn't stand under in case a falling durian hits you on the head, in which case you are likely to be knocked out, or even killed. Most hotels have signs forbidding the eating of durians because the stench, which hangs around on one's breath, as well as that of the fruit itself, puts off most western tourists.

Malaysian hotels are certainly some of the most beautiful in the world; we patronised the Shangri La and the Mandarin Oriental in Kuala Lumpur, and others, whose names I forget, in Terengganu and Malacca. Incidentally, there is a remarkable sight in an island near the coast called Pulau Tioman, about 7.20 pm each evening. This is a fly-past of enormous frigate birds going home to roost. The reason for the precise timing is that, since Malaysia is so close to the equator, sunset always occurs at the same time.

We were once taken out in Hijjas Kastouri's sailing yacht and proceeded into the Straits of Malacca, which it notable for its pirates. Thus, on another occasion, we were approached near the island of Redang on the east coast of the Malaysian peninsular (Plate 5) and stopped by a police speed boat, the officers on which thought that *we* were pirates! It took about ten minutes to persuade them that we were just tourists! Anyone who wants to know some more about pirates should read "*Lives of the Most Notorious Pirates*" by Captain Charles Johnson, published by The Folio Society in 1962. Piracy is still active to this day, mainly off the East African Coast, near Somalia.

One other unfortunate thing which happened to me in Malacca occurred on the local beach. The swimming area was delineated by a boom, to indicate where a notorious sea plant – the Crown of Thorns – had been cleared away. If you swam outside this area and trod on a Crown of Thorns, its prickles penetrated the soles of your feet, broke off and were extremely difficult to remove. I managed to avoid this catastrophe, and after my swim settled down in the shade of a tree to admire the view. Unfortunately, the sun's rays were reflected off the water on to the skin of my belly, so I got very severe and painful sunburn.

The Malaysian coast has numerous offshore islands, the largest being Penang and Langkawi to the west of the peninsula and Redang to the east. We spent time lazing around on each of these on each of these – I say 'laze', because in that hot and moist climate, any vigorous movement tends to induce profuse sweating. On the north coast of Penang is the famous beach resort of Batu Ferringhi, whose views and culinary delights we sampled. Since 1985, Penang has been connected with the mainland by a remarkable and beautiful six-lane bridge of the cable-stayed design, 13.5 kilometres long. The Works Minister responsible for its construction was Dato Samy Vellu, a good friend of the Ampi's, with whom we have dined on occasion at Mossiman's, a private dining club in London. A second, even longer bridge, connecting the south of the island to the mainland, is now being built.

One of the visits we made in Malaysia was to the Batu Caves, near Kuala Lumpur. The entrance to these caves is someway up a cliff face, and is accessed by a flight of steps at the sides of which large numbers of small and rather vicious monkeys lurk and importune visitors for nuts and other delicacies. In the cave there are colonies of bats, mainly roosting upside-down, but a few are flying around and get into your hair if you are not careful, or defaecate on you if displeased. On our most recent visit the entrance had been adorned by an enormous golden Hindu god. There is the usual array of gift shops at the bottom of the steps, with many vendors offering you their wares, which you often have to purchase to escape!

One of Ampi's concerns was the university education offered to Malaysian students. The great problem was to get into a decent university, especially if you came from a family of one of the minorities, e.g. Sri Lankan Tamil, as did Ampi and his family. The Malaysian Government was concerned that the best jobs, e.g. in medicine and the law, were being given mainly to the Indian, Sri Lankan and Chinese members of the population, because of the superior quality of their university education. They therefore instituted a quota system of university places, which strongly favoured native Malays, and it was very difficult for students of other nationalities to get accepted by a university. Ampi's solution to this was to set up a new private university, in which the Government had no right of interference. This new University – the Asian Institute of Science, Medicine and Technology (AIMST) – was initially housed in temporary accommodation at Sungai Petani, on the west coast of peninsular Malaysia, whilst its permanent buildings were being constructed at nearby Semeling. Ampi was Chairman of the Board of Governors, and I served for some time on the AIMST's International Advisory Panel. The Governors appointed the Chief Executive, who was also the Vice-Chancellor, and Barbara and I were able to put Ampi in touch with some senior people at The London who we thought might be interested in a change of scene. In this way one of the first appointees to the Chief Executive post and the Vice-Chancellorship was Fred Smales, whom we had known when he was an academic dentist at Dental Institute at The London Hospital.

When driving from Kula Lumpur to Terengganu, we climbed up Fraser's Hill and passed the spot where the British High Commissioner in Malaya, Sir Henry Gurney, was shot dead by members of the Malayan Communist Party on his way to a meeting in his Rolls Royce. Lady Gurney was with him and afterwards said that her husband had sacrificed himself to save her and his driver. His funeral was attended by many Malaysians, of all races, who seemed to have appreciated his approach to his job. The problem with terrorist guerrillas was eventually solved by the new Governor, Sir Gerald Templar; a botanic garden has been constructed in Kuala Lumpur in memory of his work.

We also spent a night in a tree house in the central Malaysian Forest (Taman Negara), which was reached by motor boat up the Tembeling River. We were armed with powerful torches with which to scan the reeds and scrub beneath us, hoping for a view of the Malaysian tiger, which declined to honour us with its presence. However, the beams of our torches only picked up a few small deer, but in the morning we saw a giant hornbill flying from one tree to another. The tiger watch reminded me of William Blake's famous lines:

"Tyger, Tyger, burning bright,
In the forest of the night;
What immortal hand or eye
Could frame thy fearful symmetry"?[1]

Curiously, the tiger appears seldom in art. The only exception which comes to mind is that by Henri 'Le Douanier' Rousseau, who frequently showed tigers in his paintings. Our sleep in that tree house was much disturbed by the continuous croaking of a small tree frog, which had taken up residence in the water tank of our arboreal residence. In the morning the motor boat returned to rescue us but matters were much delayed because the boatmen rushed off into the forest to search for durians!

House jobs

The course of training prescribed by The General Medical Council (GMC) started with House Physician and House Surgeon jobs; my House Physician posts were with Professor Clifford Wilson at The London, and Dr. Jack Ledingham, Reader in Medicine – who later succeeded Clifford Wilson on the latter's retirement. I didn't seem to be very popular with the Sister on Clifford Wilson's ward, Margaret Culpeck. One day she and I were trying to deal with a difficult patient, when John Blandy, who later became Professor of Urology, walked past. She said in a loud voice "There, Mr. Cohen, was someone who was a good Medical Unit House Physician!" Years later, at some reunion, I reminded her of this episode, which she stoutly denied ever having taken place, declaring "I would never have said a thing like that!" Jack Ledingham's laboratory on the second floor had an air-conditioning unit in the window, the outside sill of which was a roosting place for innumerable pigeons, and their fleas used to get in through the air-conditioner. They found that Jack was a very tasty morsel and bit him unmercifully! One day I entered the laboratory to find the Chief Technician, Clifford Browning, shaking DDT down Jack's trousers. They tried putting some nasty sticky paste on the window ledges, the idea being that the pigeons wouldn't like treading in it, but it never seemed to work. On one occasion, a pigeon actually got into the air conditioner, which resulted in an awful mixture of pigeon feathers, eggs and body parts flying into the lab! I have to admit that two of my favourite dishes are roast pigeon and scrambled eggs, but whenever I am eating them, I am reminded of the above dire events! Pigeons, of course, plague the major cities of the world. A notable site for this infestation is Trafalgar Square, where, in spite of notices forbidding the feeding of the pigeons, there used to be vendors (now banned) of pigeon feed present who plied a brisk trade with the tourists. There is usually a pigeon sitting on the top of the statue of Horatio Nelson, desecrating this national hero.

There was another hazard for junior doctors who had been called to see patients who had walked into the Casualty Department (known at The London as the Receiving Room). This was the high chance of acquiring some unpleasant disease or infestation from the patients, since bathing facilities for 'down and outs' were but rudimentary in the local doss houses. On one occasion, I was summoned to see an old tramp with a cough. I began to examine the chest when I noticed a number of arthropods crawling up and down over the man's sternum. Furthermore, the poor man was very embarrassed by the extra fauna he had imported, and kept on picking the body lice up, one by one, and throwing them away. I did my best to dodge these missiles, but not very successfully, since when I went to put on my white coat the following morning, there they were, crawling up and down the seams!

One evening, soon after the events related in the last paragraph, I was called to see a patient with a very extensive, almost confluent, blistering rash. To my horror, the first thing that came to mind was that the man (a sailor) had smallpox. So I ordered the Receiving Room to be locked so that no-one could get in or out, and also for the hospital doors to be closed, to minimise the chances of creating an epidemic of smallpox, not seen since the days of Edward Jenner. Thus well-patients could not be discharged and neither could their loved ones visit them. I then did my duty by summoning the local Medical Officer of Health (for overseas readers, this official was responsible for preventing the spread of infection in his district, and for making annual reports on the general health of his clientele). In due course, this official turned up and declared that he would demonstrate to me that this was not a case of smallpox, and that I had unreasonably got him out of bed. He produced a list of ten criteria for the diagnosis of smallpox, and, by the time he had got to the ninth, had gone slightly green, since they were all positive so far. He then rather meekly said that he had better get hold of a real expert. So he phoned The London School of Tropical Medicine and Hygiene, and got hold of someone who actually knew what he was doing. When this guy arrived, he took one look at the patient and said "Rubbish – if this was smallpox, the patient wouldn't be sitting up smiling with a rash as bad as that, he'd be dead by now! This is hydroa aestivale" So the whole institution was unlocked and life returned to normal. Hydroa aestivale, otherwise known as actinic prurigo, is a condition provoked by ultra-violet light. Most patients with the condition live at relatively high altitudes, where the UV light from the sun has not been largely absorbed by the Earth's atmosphere. Our sailor patient had probably got the condition as a result of unfiltered UV exposure on the high seas. It can be treated with steroid creams, and in some cases, thalidomide.

Returning for a moment to the GMC, I was once a member of the President's Advisory Committee, and, during the proceedings of one meeting, I felt a pain develop in my left big toe joint. I thought at first that this was the result of having tripped rather violently over a badly set paving stone on my way to the meeting. However, the pain got worse and worse and eventually I consulted my rheumatologist colleague at The London, Colin Barnes, who immediately diagnosed acute gout, a diagnosis that was supported by the finding that I had a raised plasma level of urate, which is the offending substance deposited in the bones, joints and soft tissues in this condition. This should not have surprised me very much, since my father suffered from painless chronic gout. Urate deposits are not opaque to X-rays, so they appear as holes in X-rays of the bones of the hands and feet, and my father's hand X-rays were riddled with holes (a hereditary element in the pathogenesis of gout is well described). My father could have written on a blackboard with his knuckles, as though they were pieces of chalk!

One of the GMC's functions was to make sure that medical schools had suitable curricula and severe enough examinations to enable licensure for medical practice. This applied both to UK medical schools and to overseas medical schools. It so happened that I was asked to inspect a number of Japanese medical schools to reassure the GMC that the standard of education was up to GMC requirements, so that Japanese doctors coming to the UK could be given a licence to practice. These schools were in Tokyo and Hamamoto on the east coast and Nagasaki and Fukuoka on the west coast. I travelled across the island from east to west in a Japanese 'bullet train' and thought that we would get a view of the beautiful Japanese countryside. Not a bit of it! The Japanese landscape is rather mountainous, and the only place where the industry can take place is in the valleys between the mountains. The valleys are therefore heavily urbanised. The local religion is mainly Shintoism and there are numerous Shinto temples in each of the towns. In them you find Shinto priests banging huge gongs, often by swinging large tree trunks, suspended horizontally by ropes, into the gong.

The Japs thought it was wise to ask me to give a lecture on a subject of my choice at each school during my visit. I duly did so and after one of the lecture was confronted by two Japanese female medical students. They both bowed and said "Professor Cohen, we were deeply honoured to be present at your honourable lecture" and proceeded to ask some questions about the topic, which were easy enough to answer. The ceremony of bowing is deeply engrained in Japanese etiquette and it is evident that the depth of the bow is determined by the social standing of the person being bowed to. The lower that standing, the more deeply you have to bow, so you can learn a lot about the status of the bowers by observing the depth to which each bows. Another curious piece of etiquette is seen at ceremonial dinners; at these, a geisha girl stands behind each guest and, when their charge takes a sip from the glass of saki initially provided, the geisha immediately refills it. So, by the end of the meal, you have absolutely no idea how much of this powerful hooch you have consumed, and it only becomes evident when you try to stand up at the end of the meal. At the end of one such ceremonial meal, the man sitting next to me threw back his head and started snoring loudly. I thought this was incredibly ill-mannered but, again, I was quite wrong. This is apparently the polite thing to do to show appreciation of the meal! Tokyo is dominated by the Imperial Palace, the home of the Emperor, otherwise known as the Mikado, from whom Gilbert and Sullivan no doubt got their inspiration for their operetta of that name. Towering over Tokyo is the snow-capped peak of Mount Fujiyama, of which I got an even better view from the plane on the flight home. The avenues in Tokyo are lined with ginkgo trees (otherwise known as maidenhair trees) which date back into prehistory for at least 270 million years. We have one in our garden in East Dean and it is thriving. Extracts of ginkgo are said to improve one's memory[2,3] and should therefore be used by absent-minded professors! It is also said to be effective in the dementia of *Alzheimer's disease[2,3], and a randomised controlled trial has provided some evidence for this assertion. There has also been some contrary evidence in other trials. So I would not advise all those with failing mental powers to rush to their local herbalist!

After my House Physician job, I became a House Surgeon to Professor Victor Dix, the Professor of Surgery (a well-known urological surgeon) on the Academic Surgical Unit. One of my tasks was to assist in the private wing (Fielden House) when Dix had a patient there. Academic clinicians in those days were permitted to see private patients, though the fees received had to go into the College's coffers, rather than into one's own pocket. I remember once assisting Victor Dix at an adult circumcision which, unlike the Jewish ceremony performed on the eighth day of life by a person known in Hebrew as a '*mowel*' and specially accredited by the *Beth Din*, is quite a substantial operation. On the occasion in question, my job was to hold out the foreskin, so that Dix could cut it off and suture the bleeding edges. I bent over somewhat in order to perform my allotted task, which caused my glasses to fall off, and they landed across the extended member. The nurses present were consumed by fits of the giggles, and Victor Dix declared "Well, I have never seen anything like that in my life!" The theatre in which Dix operated had a student's gallery, not a very good idea, since it was impossible to see in detail anything that was going on inside the group of doctors and nurses that was bending over the incision. One morning, whilst operating, we heard a cooing noise coming from the gallery – a couple of pigeons had got in through the window and were watching the operation with apparently intelligent interest! The lowly House Surgeon's usual job was to pull on a retractor, which, for instance, in the case of operations for gall stones, was inserted under the right rib cage, so that the surgeon could get a better view of the gall bladder and bile ducts, the anatomy of which was both complex and variable. On one occasion, after about an hour of such continuous activity in the hot and humid theatre, I felt faint and actually passed out on the theatre floor. I recovered consciousness to find the theatre Sister slapping me about the face with a wet towel and declaring "I haven't had a man on the floor for a long time!"

The London had a galaxy of notable orthopaedic surgeons. One of the most famous was Sir Reginald Watson-Jones, who had written the definitive textbook on fractures orthopaedic surgery. One day I was watching a hip replacement operation, the first stage of which is to make an incision over the old hip, and dislocate the joint so that access could be gained to the socket (the acetabulum) into which the ball-like head of the femur was normally inserted. Suddenly Watson-Jones turned to me and shouted "Block me, boy!" I hadn't the faintest idea what he meant, but just then the formidable head theatre sister, Miss Latham, entered the room and put me out of my misery by showing me what to do. The dislocation of the hip required considerable force, which was difficult because one's surgical boots kept on slipping on the marble floor, and they needed some firm object (in this case, my foot) on which to gain purchase to allow the manoeuvre to be performed. Watson-Jones only occasionally appeared at The London, because of the distractions of his Harley Street practice. On one of these occasions he was dragged almost by the scruff of his neck into the theatre by Miss Latham, who shouted "Now, Reggie, I won't have any of this nonsense. Go and do your job!"

It was Reggie's practice to invite all the students at the end of each firm to his home at Hindhead in Sussex for liquid refreshment. On such days, the firm was usually conveyed by bus to this village, but Barbara, who lived at West Byfleet (near

Hindhead) said she would make her own way. At the last minute, the occasion was cancelled because Reggie was in bed with a cold. The students got the message and the bus trip was cancelled, but Barbara did not receive it. When no one met her at the station, she phoned the house and was collected by a chauffeur-driven limousine. She was greeted by Reggie in his dressing gown, and was plied with an enormous amount of food and drink. She eventually got back home slightly the worse for wear!

These sorts of hang-ups in arrangements are, of course, quite common. For example, my father, who trained at The London, told me the following story. One year, the London Hospital rugby football team managed to get into the finals of the London Medicals Schools Rugby Football Cup competition, which were to be played at a sports ground in Richmond, on the other side of the city from The London Hospital. The London students were conveyed *en masse* in five coaches from the East End to Richmond. The front bus contained our mascot, some enormous teddy bear (or was it a gorilla – I can't quite remember). About a mile short of Richmond the procession was held up at a set of traffic lights. At the next change, the leading coach got across, but the lights changed again before the remaining four coaches could follow. The consequence was that the front coach arrived at Richmond alone, its passengers set upon by the opposing team in overwhelming numbers and the sacred mascot torn apart! I forget what the result of the match was, but I expect we lost. A good deal of pleasant behaviour went on from the touch line on those occasions, usually taking the form of throwing bags of gentian violet at the opposite side!

At the time when I was a student, the Professor of Pathology was a formidable lady, Dorothy Russell. We were required to attend a certain number of autopsies as part of our training, and I well remember her meticulous and pontifical style. She would, for instance, extract the liver from the body, have it weighed to the nearest gram and then start describing the surface in minute detail, e.g. "It is slightly rough in places but otherwise smooth and of a colour which varies somewhat between red, yellow and brown". She would then slice into it with a knife, scrape the surface, and say whether it was smooth, slightly granular, moderately granular or highly granular. All these details were recorded by the intern in pathology, (Barbara at one time held this appointment) and the records kept forever. A good example is when uterine curettings (taken from women complaining of abnormal vaginal bleeding) arrived in the Pathology Department. Barbara's job was to shake them out of their container and massage them into a pointed heap. She then had to record the height of the heap and its diameter at the base and a description of the curettings before they were processed for histological examination.

It is not surprising that some of these tedious practices were lampooned in the annual Christmas Show put on by the junior doctors. At one of these, Frank Loeffler, who held the post of Senior Resident Accoucheur (i.e. registrar to the Department of Obstetrics and Gynaecology), and was an excellent producer of the show, appeared on the stage disguised as Dorothy Russell, and holding in his hands a male urinal, he declared in a falsetto voice that the object was "warm, open at one end, and, fortunately, closed at the other!" Incidentally, Barbara appeared in the same show, singing a song which started "Horlicks... is best taken through a sigmoidoscope!" (A sigmoidoscope is instrument is used for visual inspection of the rectum and lower part of the colon). Dorothy Russell obviously worshipped her predecessor, Hugh Maitland Turnbull, of whom a large oil painting hung in her office. When she retired she was succeeded by Israel Doniach, from the Hammersmith Hospital, who was an altogether different type of character. On his first day in post, he identified the locker allocated to him in the department, opened the door and was horrified to be confronted by a large bust of Dorothy Russell! With regard to sigmoidoscopes, one of the placements students had to do during their training was the Out-Patient Rectal Clinic. In this clinic there were about ten examination couches, separated by curtains, for the examination of patients who had complained of seeing blood in their stools. It was the job of the relevant House Surgeon to go from couch to couch, inserting a sigmoidoscope into each patient's rear end, so that someone more senior could take a look inside and make a diagnosis. Anyone standing at the entrance to the clinic would see the ranks of inserted sigmoidoscopes resembling a battery of artillery from the First World War! Incidentally, the diagnosis of blood in the stools was usually something relatively trivial, such as haemorrhoids, but was occasionally something more serious such as cancer of the rectum or sigmoid colon, or *ulcerative colitis. You couldn't see very far into the colon with a sigmoidoscope and inspection of the higher reaches of the large intestine had to await the development of the flexible colonoscope. Successful sigmoidoscopy and colonoscopy had to be preceded by meticulous bowel preparation with laxatives and enemas, to remove all of the faecal material.

When I had come to the conclusion that a patient's trouble was more in the mind than in the body, I, of course, had to summon the psychiatrists to sort matters out. One of my patients continuously uttered repetitive obscenities. I didn't think they were deliberately aimed at myself, but they certainly disturbed the other patients in the ward. This condition is called compulsive *coprolalia and is, on occasion, a manifestation of Gilles de la Tourette syndrome, which consists of physical and vocal tics, and may be a part of an obsessive-compulsive neurosis. Tourette (1857-1904) was a French neurologist, who got shot in the head by a woman who claimed that he had hypnotised her against her will. He also angered Bismarck by publishing a paper on hysteria in the German army! Wolfgang Amadeus Mozart was said to have suffered from Tourette's syndrome, though I have to say that I don't find any trace of obscenity in his music! Anyhow, the psychiatrist who responded to my calls for help was the late Sam Cohen. He and his wife Vivienne, who later moved to Israel, were keen walkers and hill climbers, and we once bumped into them when they were descending from Stac Pollaidh (anglicised as 'Stack Polly'), a mountain in the Northwest Highlands of Scotland. This is only just over 2000 feet high, and, therefore, though spectacular and of characteristic shape, does not count as a 'Munro', the name given to Scottish peaks over 3000 feet, and named for a man who climbed them all. There are some who indulge in the sport of 'Munro-bagging', the aim of which is to climb all the Munros in Scotland.

On another occasion, when I was a junior consultant, I was summoned to the private wing of The London Hospital to give advice on an Arab lady with abdominal pain. I start to examine her abdomen, but found that my examining hand was impeded by a leather garment she was wearing. It dawned on me that this was a chastity belt! I said to the attending sister:

"Nurse, take that thing off! I can't possibly examine her with that thing in the way!"

The Sister replied:

"Dr. Cohen, if you go outside the door, you will find a guard in full Arab dress, holding a nasty looking rifle. You ask him for the key of the belt!"

I quickly decided to examine the abdomen in spite of the chastity belt!

The last of my embarrassing experiences in Fielden House was when I was called to see an Arab with Paget's disease of his left shin bone because I had a special interest in this condition of mysterious origin which causes thickening of the bone. Having done my stuff and prescribed the appropriate treatment, the Arab asked me what my fee was. My usual answer for a service of this nature was £15, but, having in mind that the patient came from Kuwait, and probably owned half of this oil-rich state, I said "£25". The patient replied "Don't be ridiculous!" and proceeded to write me a cheque for £200! The reader may understand why after these experiences I decided to pursue a career in Academic Medicine and eschew the fleshpots of Harley Street!

Barbara was also a House Surgeon to Victor Dix, who specialised in dealing with men whose urine flow had been obstructed by enlargement of the prostate gland at the base of the bladder. This retention of urine is initially treated by insertion of a urinary catheter, to relieve symptoms temporarily before the definitive therapy of *prostatectomy. The story is told that each morning, Barbara would enter the ward, shut the door behind her and lean on the closed door, slowly twirling a catheter. This caused all the male patients to cringe beneath their bedclothes. Barbara also caused a stir one evening after the three-monthly Mess Dinner by dancing a jig on the billiard table. She later rushed off to the Medical School, where she heard a snoring noise coming from a large dustbin. Having lifted the lid she found the College Secretary of the day, who had also been at the Mess Dinner, sleeping it off. She quietly replaced the lid. Barbara had lodgings in a somewhat run-down house in New Road, Whitechapel. Her rooms had a rather peculiar odour, eventually identified as being due to bed bugs!

The other insect prevalent in Whitechapel was the cockroach. These creatures like warmth, which, of course, speeds up activity in cold-blooded animals. They therefore infested the basement corridors of the Hospital where the central heating pipes ran, and, as you walked along this passageway, which connected the Hospital to the Medical College, there were ominous crunching sounds underfoot. I once made a home visit to a patient with our social worker, Grace Dedman. I noticed that this hovel had what was a peculiar brown, shiny and rather expensive-looking wallpaper. Suddenly, the whole wallpaper seemed to move sideways, and we then realised that the wallpaper was, in fact, a solid mass of cockroaches, the members of which had made a sudden unanimous decision to take a walk in precisely the same direction! Cockroaches were everywhere and could be found in people's houses crawling over the babies' faces. Fortunately, these insects are not known to be vectors of any particular disease, unlike the rat flea, which carries the agent of *bubonic plague (*Pasteurella pestis*).

During my time at The London, it so happened that some builders were digging a large hole in the back garden of the hospital in order to prepare the foundations of a new building. As the diggers got deeper and deeper, eventually vanishing out of sight, the only evidence that they were still at their work was the emergence of human bones which they were flinging out of the hole. They had, in fact, struck a 'plague pit', into which corpses were thrown during the Great Plague of London in 1665. The Plague of London was part of the Black Death, which was sweeping Europe at this time. The bodies were collected by hand-drawn carts, with someone walking in front of the cart, ringing a bell and shouting "Bring out your dead!"

Clifford Wilson was as distinguished a physician as his somewhat patriarchal appearance suggested. He was especially well known for two pieces of research. Firstly, with Kimmelstiel, he identified the kidney lesion specific to patients with diabetes mellitus (now known universally as the Kimmelstiel-Wilson lesion), and, secondly, his development with Jack Ledingham and their colleague, Michael Floyer, using rats, of the discovery by Harry Goldblatt, of Western Reserve, that partial occlusion of one *renal artery in the dog, caused high blood pressure (hypertension). During my visit to Cleveland, I called upon Goldblatt, who invited me to visit his dogs. One might have thought that these animals would react aggressively to the man experimenting on them. Not a bit of it! When we entered the laboratory, the dogs rushed up to him, licked his face, and then leapt up on to the operating table and lay on their backs with their legs parted so that he could puncture their femoral arteries, and thus measure their blood pressure and obtain blood samples for laboratory analysis!

After my House Jobs I was acutely conscious that nearly all my professional time so far had been spent at The London, and I was therefore anxious to gain some wider experience. So I applied for and was appointed as House Officer to Professor Russell Fraser (known as 'Rusty'), an endocrinologist of New Zealand extraction at the Royal Postgraduate Medical School at Hammersmith Hospital in the west of London. One of our projects there was to set up a gas chromatographic technique for measuring the Krebs cycle and related intermediates in blood and tissues[4]. One of my colleagues on this enterprise was David Barnett, of whom there is more later.

Next to the Hammersmith Hospital is Wormwood Scrubs Prison, from which there have been a number of notorious escapes, notably that of George Blake in 1966. Blake was a British spy who was also a double agent for the Soviet Union. He switched sides in protest against the relentless bombing of small villages by the Americans during the Korean War. He betrayed hundreds of MI6 agents to the Soviets, but in 1961 was exposed by a Polish defector from the Soviet Communist regime and was sentenced to forty two years imprisonment. His escape was highly ingenious and employed a rope ladder constructed from knitting needles!

When I was Russell Fraser's House Physician, the hospital admitted a twenty- one month old little girl whose illness we were having great difficulty in diagnosing. The diagnosis of *thallium poisoning was suggested by a nurse, who had been reading a crime thriller by Agatha Christie entitled *"The Pale Horse"*, in which the murder was committed by poisoning with thallium. A prominent symptom was that the child's hair was falling out, and this was the symptom which led to the nurse's suggestion. Measurements of thallium in the urine were made and found to be extremely high. My colleague at the time, Professor Victor Dubowitz, learnt that an expert on thallium poisoning, a certain Graham Young, was at the time a 'guest of Her Majesty', was serving a life sentence in Wormwood Scrubs Prison. He had poisoned his parents and some other relatives, and later some of his workmates, with thallium, and was said to be an expert on the symptoms, signs and treatment of this condition. The prisoner was consulted by Dr Peter Rudge, who had studied some of Young's victims. As a result, the child was treated with oral Prussian Blue and potassium chloride and made an almost complete recovery.[5] Serendipitously, as I was drafting this account of the saga, there was a TV production of *"The Pale Horse"* that evening.

There is a radioactive isotope of thallium (thallium 201) which has been extensively used as a tool for the non-invasive diagnosis of coronary vascular disease. Thallium is taken up by the heart muscle, but if there are areas of poor perfusion, gaps appear in the image. More recently it has been replaced[16] by ^{18}F-flurpidaz, a compound of a radioactive isotope of fluorine, which provides better images.

Lectureship
1 spent six months at The Hammersmith before returning to The London as one of Clifford Wilson's Lecturers. Clifford Wilson was not very fond of lecturing, so he often used to ask me do his share of the talking for him. On every occasion when

this happened he always told me to remind the students that the kidney is the most important organ in the body! Being dutiful to my boss, and anxious for promotion, I indeed told them that "The liver is the most important organ in the body!" Clifford never, to my knowledge, found out about this piece of deception.

I also did quite a lot of research with Jack Ledingham on the role of the heart in the pathogenesis of hypertension, using rats as the experimental animal[6]. There was at this time a major controversy between Sir George Pickering at Oxford on the one hand, and Wilson, Ledingham and Floyer at The London on the other on the pathogenesis of hypertension. The background is that the flow through any pipe (an artery in the present case) is determined positively by the pressure exerted on the fluid, and negatively by the resistance to flow. Pickering believed that constriction of the smaller arteries (the arterioles) caused by the release of * renin from the juxta-glomerular apparatus of the kidney, with consequent production of the *vasoconstrictor, angiotensin, was the primary initiating cause, whereas the group at The London thought that the primary cause was an increase in cardiac output, with the peripheral arterioles constricting in response to this in order to keep the blood flow through the tissues constant, a process known as autoregulation of blood flow. Jack Ledingham and I constructed (with the help of Cliff Browning, his Chief Technician, who was an electronics expert) an electromagnetic flowmeter which could be implanted on the ascending aorta of rats, with its leads emerging at the back of the animal's neck. After the operation the rats settled quite comfortably and the cardiac output was recorded several times per day for ten days. Their blood pressure was measured by a cuff on the tail, rather like a sphygmomanometer cuff, under light ether anaesthesia and the pulse rate was obtained from the flowmeter trace. A clip (the equivalent of the Goldblatt clamp) was then placed so as to partly occlude the right renal artery, and the development of hypertension was observed daily. The ensuing rise of blood pressure was accompanied by a transient elevation of cardiac output for a few days, together with a slowing of the pulse rate (bradycardia), followed by a return to normal. This seemed to support the ideas of The London group, since, if Pickering's idea of a primary increase in peripheral resistance was right, slowing of the pulse would be expected and a fall, rather than a rise, in cardiac output would occur, due to an attempt by the pressure receptors in the aorta and carotid arteries to initiate a reflex which would reduce the cardiac output. I do not know where this controversy has got to at the present time, and it must be remembered that humans and rats may differ in their pathophysiological responses.

I also had a an early interest in kidney stones, no doubt inspired by my father's affliction described in Chapter 1. There are several types of stone, for example, calcium phosphate and oxalate stones, *cystine stones, and magnesium ammonium phosphate stones. Cystine stones are the result of an inherited metabolic abnormality of kidney *tubular *transport, and, despite both this and my father's illness, I wondered whether there was a familial (but non-genetic) element in the causation of calcium-containing stones. So, in cooperation with the urologists at The London, we did a study which showed that urinary calcium excretion and calcium stones were more common in the spouses of stone formers than in control groups of the same sex in households where no one had stones. We attributed this to the dominant member of a stone forming household having a preference for milk-containing foods, and demanding to be fed with them ("I want my milk pudding!"). When they got their way, as was usual, the non-dominant members of the household also ate milk pudding, and therefore had an increased propensity for stone formation[7].

My next research effort was related to my MD thesis of 1966[8,9], on the metabolic effects of treating *myxoedema, otherwise known as hypothyroidism. I looked after several of these patients in what was then the Metabolic Ward of The London Hospital. This was geared up for the performance of what are known as metabolic balance studies. This consisted of measuring everything that went into a patient, i.e. food, fluid, medicines and intravenous infusions, and also everything that came out, e.g. urine and faeces. If you were looking, for instance, at sodium balance, you could then subtract the output from the input of sodium and thus find out how much sodium the subject had gained over the period of the study, typically five days. The dieticians had to feed precisely the same diet each day to the patient (who had to be willing to put up with this monotony). A whole day's input was then analysed for sodium, and the total collection of urine and faeces was similarly analysed. In order to do this the food, urine and faeces had to be reduced to a clear colourless fluid, which could then be analysed for sodium in a flame photometer. This transformation was effected by digesting these solids, by boiling in concentrated perchloric acid in a fume cupboard. Now, the fume cupboard in the Metabolic Laboratory had a wooden framework, and the effect of fumes from repeated perchloric acid digestions caused the wood to rot. Perchloric acid-rotted wood is highly spontaneously inflammable, and one day the fume cupboard caught fire. The laboratory staff were rescued by the patients in the ward, who leapt out of bed and rushed in with fire extinguishers!

What actually happened in the first few days after the start of treatment of myxoedema was a massive diuresis (increased output of urine), resulting in a corresponding loss of weight, due to the jelly-like fluid in the tissues, which gave rise to the characteristic puffiness of the tissues, dispersing. For anyone interested in this phenomenon, it is easier to look it up in the paper I published in the journal *"Clinical Science"*, than finding my MD thesis, which is buried somewhere in the library of Cambridge University. (I was Chairman of the Editorial Board of Clinical Science for two years from 1973-1975, a post which involved the arduous task of keeping in order the other members of the Board, amongst whom there often was a considerable variation of opinion on what was worth publishing.)

My laboratory was on the second floor of the hospital. I always found it necessary to have a colleague working with me who was a professional biochemist, rather than an amateur one like myself, though I also had some medical colleagues in the lab as well. One of these medical colleagues was David Barnett, with whom I have fished for trout, for many years in Wharfedale, usually at Watersmeet, where the River Wharfe is joined by its tributary, the Skirfare. I trained my son Martin in the angler's art and he very soon became much better than myself, ultimately catching five fish for every one of mine. Though the acme of an angler's experience is to be so in tune with nature that a kingfisher alights on the tip of one's rod, this never happened to me. There are also many down-sides; firstly, trout tend to rise and take fishing flies at dawn and in the gloaming at night, an inconvenient fact which, in the morning, disturbs one's beauty sleep, and in the evening makes one late for dinner. In addition, Barbara and David's wife, Angela, who did not fish, got very bored sitting on the bank watching us. However, they bravely put up with this and brought us our lunch, usually beef sandwiches. The next down-side is having to wear waders which are difficult to get on and off. Also, whilst wading into the river to reach a suitable vantage point, one occasionally tripped over and got thoroughly soaked, despite the use of a special device known at a wading stick.

The next issue is the question of bait; we always used fishing flies, and the loading of the barb of the hook with something like a piece of worm or a maggot was eschewed, being regarded as unsporting. Much effort is expended in selecting an appropriate fly. The true expert slowly approaches the river, notes whether the fish are rising to fly, and if so the type of fly. He then ties a fly to imitate the prevalent variety. I couldn't be bothered with all this rigmarole, so I used to buy a variety of flies from fishing shops e.g. Greenwell's Glory, Grey Duster, and Claret and Purple, and hope that one from my fly box would suit the local conditions. The next problem is whether to fish upstream or downstream, i.e. in which direction to cast one's line. If the fish are rising to fly, as identified by the circular pattern of ripples after a rise (caused by a fish poking its nose out of the water to catch a fly wandering by, then upstream fishing is the best technique. If there are no hatches of flies, and, therefore, no rises, then the downstream approach is appropriate, using a sinking line. This is first cast across the river and allowed to sweep round in an arc, whilst one gradually pulls in the line. At the slightest tremor felt down the line one quickly strikes by elevating the rod, and, with luck, you have hooked a fish, which then proceeds to fight like mad, and it is essential to keep the line taut whilst bringing the catch in, else it might escape by waggling its head. Having hopefully netted the fish, you bash it over the head with an instrument ironically known as a 'priest', and then proceed to the sordid business of gutting it via an abdominal incision. Despite all this trouble, there is nothing like the taste of freshly caught and grilled trout for breakfast.

We have also fished for trout, with only minor success, in Loch Harray in the island of Orkney, off the north coast of Scotland. The journey requires a usually pretty rough crossing of the Pentland Firth. The lady who was the proprietor of the Merkister Hotel flew her own seaplane weekly to the mainland to purchase supplies with which to feed her guests. Martin caught the only fish of the week, which the hotel kitchen managed to overcook! Orkney also contains a number of Viking remains and burial grounds, notably at the village of Scara Brae. I have only fished for salmon on one occasion, on the River Deveren in Aberdeenshire, North East Scotland. In this case the only success was catching a fairly large fish, the bait being a collection of glittering metal attached to the line just above the hook. The fish only took me about ten minutes to land and weighed about seven pounds; sometimes, with a really large fish, it can take an hour to get the catch into the take net, and occasionally the angler gets pulled into the drink! I was once invited to fish at a well-known establishment known as Two Lakes, fairly near to Southampton, which seems to be used largely by peers of the realm. For their convenience, special platforms jutting out out into the lake had been erected to stand on whilst fishing, and it was obvious to me that the anglers were pulling in enormous fish every two or three minutes, the maximum catch allowed per rod being two per session. I thought this was a bit curious, so I walked around a bit and found a river bailiff letting in an enormous fish from a fish farm every time he saw that one of his clients had hooked a fish. He declared that

"Their Lordships like to catch a lot of fish".

C'est magnifique, mais ce n'est pas le sport!

My first laboratory scientific colleague was Richard Iles, with whom I wrote thirteen papers between 1970 and 1985. Richard later became a Professor of Biochemistry, specialising in magnetic resonance spectrometry (MRS), which may be used to measure the concentration of certain metabolites in body fluids and tissues, notably compounds containing phosphorus, hydrogen, carbon and fluorine. One of our interests was the measurement of the pH within cells (pH_i), because it seemed to us that since most biochemical reactions, many of which are pH-dependent, take place inside cells rather than outside, this was the place to look when trying to determine what was regulating the rate of biochemical processes. At this time, two American scientists, WJ Waddell and TC Butler[10], had developed a method for measuring intracellular pH, which depended on the distribution of an inert non-toxic weak acid dimethyl oxazolidine 2,4-dione (DMO) across cell membranes. The method depended on the fact that the cell membrane is permeable to the lipid-soluble unionised form (DMO), but completely impermeable to the ionised form (DMO⁻).

Thus, if the subscripts 'e' and 'i' represent the extra- and intracellular compartments respectively, H the hydrogen ion concentration, I and U the concentrations of the ionised and unionised fractions, K the dissociation constant of DMO, R the total DMO concentration in the compartment designated by the subscripts, V the volume of the compartment and W the total amount of DMO added to the system, we have, at equilibrium, from the Law of Mass Action, the following relationships:

$$H_e I_e / U_e = K = H_i I_i / U_i \dots\dots\dots\dots (1)$$
$$R_e = I_e + U_e \text{ and } R_i = I_i + U_i \dots\dots\dots\dots (2)$$

Combining these equations,

$$U_e = H_e R_e / (K + H_e) \text{ and } U_i = H_i R_i / (K + H_i) \dots\dots\dots (3)$$

Since at equilibrium $U_e = U_i$, it follows that

$$H_i = H_e R_e (K+H_i)/R_i(H+H_e) \dots\dots\dots\dots\dots\dots\dots\dots\dots (4)$$

Since $W = V_e R_e + V_i R_i$, by inserting this into (4) we have:-
$$H_i = R_e H_e K/\{(W/V_i - V_e R_e/V_i)([K+H_e] - R_e H_e\}$$

Because everything on the right hand side of this equation is known or easily measureable, it is possible to calculate the intracellular pH (pH_i). However, these were the days before The London Hospital possessed a computer, and all the calculations had to be performed using slide rules. My colleagues and I spent many nights making these calculations at my home, sustained by beer and fried eggs supplied by Barbara.

One of the tasks a cell has to perform is to regulate its internal pH at a reasonably steady level, except when circumstances demand otherwise. There are three possible methods at its disposal. The first is simple buffering by the *cytosol, for instance by interconversion of monophosphate and diphosphate ions, i.e.

$$HPO_4^{2-} + H^+ \rightleftharpoons H_2PO_4^{1-}$$

Another is the active extrusion of unwanted H^+ through the cell membrane, by means of a *proton pump requiring energy, e.g. from adenosine triphosphate (ATP). The last method is by metabolism of the ionised form of a weak acid to a neutral product, e.g. glucose or carbon dioxide and water. To take the case of lactate, we have:

$$2CH_3CHOHCOO^- + 2H^+ \rightarrow glucose$$
lactate

The H^+ ions on the left hand side of this equation are effectively obtained from water:

$$2H_2O \rightarrow 2H^+ + 2OH^-$$

This is followed by:

$$2OH^- + 2CO_2 \rightarrow 2HCO_3^-$$

It may be seen that hydrogen ions are consumed in this process and bicarbonate ions generated. Thus the liver cell is alkalinised during *gluconeogenesis, in proportion to the rate at which it takes place.

Since we were interested in the relationship between extracellular *pH (pH_e) and intracellular pH (pH_i), we did a series of studies to establish this relationship under a variety of conditions in isolated rat liver perfused with sodium lactate as the substrate. We showed that as pH_e was lowered from its mean normal value of about 7.4 to the highly acidotic value of 6.7, pH_i did indeed fall, but much more slowly. There was no change in lactate uptake until pH_i had fallen below 7.05; thereafter there was a dramatic reversal from lactate uptake to lactate output.

One memorable incident during the studies I have described above was that the extraction of DMO from the tissue extract involved shaking it with chloroform, and during the process our rather attractive laboratory scientific officer managed to spill a large amount of chloroform, which soaked through her white coat and got on to her dress, which was made of some synthetic fabric which was soluble in chloroform. It was clear that her dress had been ruined. I sent her over to the Domestic Bursar to claim compensation, and by the time she had got to his office, she was almost down to her underwear. She opened her white coat to show him the damage, and, during her return journey, the Domestic Bursar called me and said in a hoarse voice: "You can send me more of those any time you like!" The College paid for the damage!

The principle of non-ionic diffusion is also employed in the treatment of aspirin poisoning. We had a patient who had swallowed 300 aspirin tablets which, overall, contained 90g of salicylate, a weak acid. The procedure is known as 'forced alkaline diuresis', which consists of infusion, in rotation, of sodium bicarbonate, sodium chloride and 5% dextrose solutions. In this case we administered twelve litres of these solutions over a period of fourteen hours, and the blood salicylate level fell from the enormous value of 138 mg/100 ml to 15 mg/100 ml, which is in the ordinary therapeutic range used for pain relief. The purpose of achieving such high flow rates is to achieve the largest possible diffusion gradient for the undissociated moiety of acetyl salicylic acid (aspirin) between the blood and the renal tubular urine. Because this was possibly the severest case ever successfully treated by this method, we published a report on the management of this case in the *British Medical Journal*[11].

We also went through other methods for measuring cell pH, including the insertion of double-barrelled microelectrodes. We were shown the technique of making these by Roger Thomas, of the University of Bristol. Their manufacture was technically very difficult, and the end product was very fragile. However, despite this, we did manage one project using this technique which was publishable[12]. In this we showed that the mean intracellular pH (likely to be cytosol pH) in the renal tubules of lightly anaesthetised rats was 7.1, and the mean potential in the part of the tubular cell membrane on the opposite side of the tubule to its lumen was -51.8 mV. We also showed that the cytosol pH was much more alkaline than would be expected if hydrogen ions (H^+) were in diffusion equilibrium across the renal tubular cell membrane. This implied that H^+ was either being pumped out at one or both of the luminal or basolateral membranes, or, alternatively, bicarbonate or hydroxyl ions were being pumped in. Anyone reading this paper will be put off from contemplating using the technique by the great complexity of the technical arrangements needed, which included an extremely heavy marble table to insulate the experiments from small vibrations caused by walking around the laboratory and the constant flow of heavy lorries in the Whitechapel Road outside.

Fortunately, the whole situation was revolutionised by the development of magnetic resonance spectrometry (MRS), and there was a suitable spectrometer just down the road at Queen Mary College. The great advantage of this technique is that it is totally non-invasive; there is no destruction or damage to the subject within the spectrometer and the measurements can be repeated with impunity. I have had myself inserted into a spectrometer and felt no discomfort whatsoever, except that my arms went numb. I then realized that I had forgotten to remove the metallic arm bands I was wearing to hold up the sleeves of my shirt, which were slightly too long! There were initial fears that the brain might be damaged by the oscillating magnetic field used, but these proved unfounded. The technique uses a property of the nuclei of the phosphorus atoms in a compound, and, in this case, an object (such as myself (!)) placed in the spectrometer. This equipment consists of large magnetic coils, energised by an electric current, producing a very strong, stable and homogeneous field. When subjected to a series of pulses of magnetic field at a frequency specific to phosphorus, the nuclei of the phosphorus atoms, which have both a positive charge and spin, behave like tiny magnets and oscillate from side to side, at a frequency proportional to the magnetic field strength. The frequency is influenced by the electron cloud that binds neighbouring atoms together to form molecular compounds, causing a shift in the frequency of oscillation (the 'chemical shift') dependent on the precise nature of the local chemical environment. When the magnetic field declines at the end of each oscillation cycle, the nuclei relax from the disturbance at a characteristic rate and the energy absorbed during the initial disturbance is released as electromagnetic radiation. An example is the spectrum of adenosine triphosphate (ATP) at pH 7.0. This shows three peaks, one for each of the phosphorus atoms of ATP. A graph can be plotted of the variation of the chemical shift with pH, and thus, the pH can be read off. It so happens that the relaxation of phosphorus in the extracellular space is much slower than that in the intracellular space and, if the frequency of the pulses is appropriately chosen, there is no perceptible relaxation in the signal from the extracellular space, thus, the relaxation that is detectable is entirely from the intracellular space; this is the fundamental basis of the selectivity of measurement of intracellular pH by this method. The relaxation is detected from the signal induced in a small coil placed around the part of the body of interest e.g. the brain or liver. It is not necessary to make an incision to insert the detection coil; placing the coil on the skin over the target organ is all that is necessary. The various signals in the record are separated out by *Fourier transformation. Lastly, a lot of 'noise' is generated in the experiment; this is eliminated by repeating the basic experiment many times (e.g. 300) in rapid succession, and superimposing the results to improve the signal to noise ratio. Richard Iles became expert at this technique, co-authoring a book on the subject[6].

After we had published a paper or two using the MRS technique, I was invited to join a Medical Research Council (MRC) grants committee that dealt with grant applications in my field. The procedure for selecting which applications to fund was quite complicated. Before each meeting you were sent thirty or forty applications to go through at home and decide which you were going to recommend at the subsequent committee meetings at MRC headquarters in Portland Crescent near Regents Park. You spoke about each of the applications allocated to you for about ten minutes, describing the project and giving your view of its merits and demerits. There were two lead speakers on each project, and at the end of the presentation, and taking into account points raised by other members of the committee, each member of the committee scored the application from one to ten. The scores for each project were added up and arranged in order of magnitude, with the amount of funding applied for noted in the margin. A line was drawn where the available money ran out, and all projects above that line were funded. A good deal of application 'pruning' went on in the committee, reducing the sums allocated, perhaps on the basis that it was partly unnecessary, that you didn't need two technicians because one would do, or that the item ought to be paid for by the institute or medical school from which the application originated. This pruning often meant that borderline applications could be supported. At the time when I was a member of a Grants Committee (1985-1988), it was felt to be essential that a project application should be for work which supported or refuted a hypothesis or theory, and not just for surveys – for example, of the prevalence of athlete's foot in Rutlandshire – in the hope that some interesting findings or ideas would arise from such an exercise. That sort of application was damned as 'a fishing expedition' and, once someone had made such piscatorial allusions, the application was almost certainly doomed to be rejected. These Grants Committees only dealt with applications for single project funding, whereas those for suites of related projects ('programme grants') were dealt with at one level higher up at Board level. I became a member of the Board which dealt with physiological systems and the diseases affecting them from 1990-1992. The various Research Councils, (the MRC, the Biotechnology and Biological Sciences Research Council, the Engineering and Physical Sciences Research Council, the Arts and Humanities Research Council, the Natural Environment Research Council, the Science and Technical Facility Research Council and the Economic and Social Research Council), distributed the money allocated to them by the Advisory Board for Research Councils (now known as Research Councils UK). These funds ultimately derived from the Government's annual Science Vote. The above constellation of research councils represents the current situation and, so far as my memory serves me, was slightly different when I was in post.

When I was on the MRC, it was customary to appoint various members of the Grants Committees and Boards to various more ephemeral subcommittees. One of these was the MRC Virucides Steering Committee. The remit of this body was to encourage the development of a vaginal preparation which would prevent the entry of human immuno-deficiency virus (HIV) through the mucosa of the vagina. The idea was to help women protect themselves in circumstances when their male partners refused to use condoms. Substances under test from 2002 included dextrin sulphate and PRO 2000. The latter has proved to be ineffective, at least at the concentrations used in the vaginal gel. Dextrin sulphate is a polyanion which blocks entry of HIV into the vaginal epithelial cell, and is, to the best of my knowledge, still under trial in the UK, Belgium and Uganda. It has been important to be able to show that dextrin sulphate does not set up an inflammation of the vaginal mucosa which might actually facilitate entry of the virus. Another consideration is that such a substance should not be spermicidal. PRO 2000 and dextrin sulphate are by no means the only substances which have been tried in this context; for instance, nonoxynol-9, had no side effects but did not prevent transmission of HIV.

I was also sent by the Department of Health (DoH) to Canada as a member of the committee which distributed grants for infrastructure to academic medical departments in Canada. The downside of this task was that it took place in Ottawa, which must be one of the most boring capital cities in the world! There is an amusing story in this context, namely, that at Heathrow, where I was due to catch a flight to Canada in a routine British Airways Boeing 747, something went wrong with the aircraft and the passengers were left stranded in the departure lounge. The DoH has a rather surprising rule that their staff of the rank of Assistant Secretary or above on a journey lasting more than two hours, always travelled first class, and with them, any accompanying Board members, because it would be somewhat embarrassing to have the DoH official upstairs in the first class accommodation, leaving their companions stranded in economy class. So I and the Assistant Secretary were transferred to a Concorde flight, in which the seating was entirely first-class. Concorde was the world's first supersonic aircraft, jointly developed by Britain and France, and cut the usual Heathrow to New York journey time from 5.5 to about 3.5 hours. The cabin was divided into two sections, each of which had at the front of it a Machmeter, which gave the aircraft's relation to the speed of sound; thus Mach 0.7 is subsonic, whereas Mach 1.3 is supersonic. From where I was sitting in the front of the rear section, both Machmeters were visible so it was somewhat disconcerting to find that the front meter read 1.3, whilst the rear meter showed 1.2. I looked to see if the plane was coming apart in the middle, but since this was manifestly not the case, I concluded that the discrepancy was due to instrumental error. The cabin crew looked after you exceptionally well during the flight, providing you with slippers in which to pad about the aircraft. The meals were remarkable; I was served with a deliciously cooked rare beefsteak, washed down with my favourite wine, Chateau Léoville Lascases, of an exceptionally good vintage. On the flight I bought Barbara a superb blue, pink and white silk scarf with the Concorde logo on it. During the flight those who were first time Concorde fliers were invited to visit the flight deck, where the co-pilot showed us dials which indicated that we were flying at 59,000 ft – almost in the stratosphere, and that the outside temperature was -30°C. In response to the co-pilot's query whether there was anything else I would like to know, I asked how they knew precisely where we were. The co-pilot then showed me an illuminated colour screen of the Atlantic, superimposed upon which a moving red spot was indicating our location. The only downside to this adventure was that when we landed in New York, I found that my baggage had not been transferred to Concorde and was on the original flight on which I had been scheduled to travel, which was bound for Philadelphia. However, my baggage and I were soon reunited.

Our house in Beckenham was immediately under the Concorde flight path and we frequently got excellent views of this striking aircraft from our garden. Unfortunately, shortly after this an Air France Concorde crashed soon after take-off in Paris, due to a fuel tank being punctured by a piece of debris thrown up from the runway, and all six Concordes were permanently withdrawn from service. I was never quite sure of all the reasons for this seemingly harsh decision, but some of the factors may have been public protest against the sonic boom emitted as the aircraft went through the sound barrier, and the high fuel consumption costs. For many years, one of the Concordes stood on the lawn at the entrance to the tunnel leading into Heathrow Airport. Our journey back from the USA was unfortunately on a much more mundane Boeing 747 flight.

The other source of funding for my personal research was The Wellcome Trust. There was a feeling that if one had to accept money from pharmaceutical companies, it provided lesser kudos for the future development of one's career, since the applications were not so rigorously refereed as those sent to the Research Councils, and there was always a suspicion that the drug companies were using you to promote their own products. The Wellcome Trust was, however, free from these suspicions. It had been set up originally by Sir Henry Wellcome, a tycoon who used the funds from his drug company (Burroughs Wellcome – the Wellcome Foundation) to fund the Wellcome Trust. The latter was therefore at arm's length from the business and was therefore unlikely to be affected in its grant-giving activities by commercial considerations.

Because of my known interest in MRS I was invited in 1968 to chair the Medical Research Council/Department of Health and Social Security Committee on Magnetic Resonance Imaging (MRI). MRI, which produces elegant pictures of cross-sections of the body, is a slightly different technique to spectroscopy, but the basic principles are the same.[13] This position involved making visits to the MRC funded MRI unit (led by Peter Mansfield in Nottingham) and the MRS Unit headed by George Radda in Oxford.

Peter Mansfield had developed a technique which he named 'echoplanar MRI', which was designed to produce images in real time. They invited me to get into the bore of his machine, and I had the eerie experience of seeing my own brain pulsating with each heartbeat. MRI and MRS machines at that time consisted of coils super-cooled in liquid helium (to bring them to a state where their electrical resistance was almost zero). The metallic elements around which the coils were wound vibrated, creating a loud noise which added to one's general discomfort. The powerful magnetic field grabs anything magnetic and this can be dangerous, let alone wiping out credit cards etc. In fact, these machines are surrounded by a red line beyond which no ferromagnetic objects may be taken. There was an episode when a cleaner accidentally pushed her vacuum cleaner into the forbidden zone. The gadget was instantly sucked on to the magnet, and the cleaner was somewhat bruised whilst desperately trying to hold on!

Fairly early in my career, I obtained the Membership of the Royal College of Physicians (without which it was virtually impossible to get appointed to a Consultant Physician post), and later the Fellowship. Some years later I became Senior Censor and First Vice-President, and as such had to sit with the notables invited to the College's most important day of each year, William Harvey Day, when a distinguished speaker gives the 'Harveian Oration' which was followed by a sumptuous dinner. It so happened that at one such dinner I was placed next to Kenneth Clarke, who was Secretary of State for Health at the time and responsible for funding the Medical Research Council, which then distributed the cash to the best research grant applicants in the way I have outlined above. During the meal he asked me, in his forthright fashion,

'"Who was this bloke Harvey, anyway?"

So I told him about Harvey's discovery of the circulation ("*De Motu Cordis,* 1628), and stripped my sleeve (as did Henry V at the Battle of Agincourt) and repeated for him Harvey's demonstration of the circulation of the blood. Before Harvey did his stuff, it was generally believed that the blood flowed to and fro with each heartbeat in both arteries and veins. Harvey's experiment showed, by exerting pressure on the veins in the forearm, that they only refilled from the direction of the hand, and therefore were involved only in returning blood to the heart for re-oxygenation in the lungs. After my demonstration Kenneth Clarke commented

"Quite clever, that! At least he didn't demand a bloody research grant!"

This remark ensured that I did not suggest to him that the Science Vote should be increased!

During most of my time as Senior Censor, the President of the College was Margaret Turner-Warwick. She was a well-known respiratory physician, and the first woman to become President, such had been the general male chauvinism over the past few hundred years of the College's existence. Every month, she held a meeting (the PBD – Presidential Business Discussion) of the senior College officers to plan the College's activities for the next few months. Dinner was served at this meeting, accompanied by the finest wines from the College's cellars. On one of these occasions I slipped out of the Censors' Room, where the meetings were held, tracked down the College catering supervisor and managed to extract from her the name and vintage of the wine due to be served. When it came to drinking some of it, I sipped it, swilled it around my mouth as do the real pundits, turned to the Treasurer, Norman Jones (a physician at St. Thomas's Hospital, who was responsible for the suitable stocking of the wine cellar) and said "Ah! The Chateau Branaire, 1975" which was of course, precisely what it was. Norman Jones turned green at this display of oenological expertise, but after a few minutes he turned to me and shouted

"Cheat!"

He was, however, so impressed by my keenness that he put me on the College Wine Committee, which met every few months under the supervisor of a genuine Master of Wine, Derek Smedley, to decide what the College would buy for its cellars. I spent a happy twelve years on this Committee (? the most important and influential in the College), and, of course, the wines were paid for by the annual subscriptions of the general Fellowship and Membership, who, I trust, were satisfied with the use to which their money was being put!) before I decided to resign to give someone else a chance. Each member of the Committee was allowed to take home one unfinished bottle from amongst those we had tasted – it was usually still about three-quarters full. Barbara was usually waiting for me in the car after these meetings, and woe betide me if I had not brought with me most of a bottle of some delicious vintage!

In the early 1970's I was summoned by one of my colleagues, John Ward, to see a man aged thirty-six with severe acidosis. He had renal failure due to chronic *glomerulonephritis, and had abnormal glucose tolerance. For this he was treated with the biguanide drug, phenformin, and after eight days of treatment he began to vomit and developed the deep sighing respiration known as *Kussmaul breathing, a characteristic phenomenon in severe acidosis. He proved to have a high blood lactate level (28.4 mmol/l, compared with the normal level of up to 1 mmol/l) and a low blood pH of 7.2 (normal range 7.37-7.42). He was treated with sodium bicarbonate – a therapy discussed later – and haemodialysis, to speed removal of the phenformin. I saw a second case of phenformin-induced lactic acidosis in a boy aged seventeen who had swallowed 30-40 phenformin capsules, containing a total of 1500-2000 mg of the drug at 6 p.m. on the day before admission, presumably with suicidal intent. By 8.30 the next morning, he was unconscious, with Kussmaul breathing, and an arterial blood pH of 7.08. He eventually died, without recovering consciousness. Both patients had low blood partial pressures of carbon dioxide, due to the hyperventilation, a normal means of compensation when one lowers one's blood pH by generating lactic acid anaerobically during vigorous exercise. Both patients also had normal blood pressures and had warm, well-perfused extremities, in contrast to the cold hands due to vasoconstriction seen in shock, due to, for instance, uncontrolled haemorrhage. Accounts of these cases were reported to The Committee on Safety of Medicines. Shortly afterwards, the use of phenformin and its congener, buformin, mainly used in Germany, was stopped. However, the use of metformin, another congener, was not stopped, because it was clear that there was much less risk of lactic acidosis with this medication. In a review of the literature[14], I found that metformin was about thirteen times less likely than phenformin to cause lactic acidosis per unit duration of therapy. Metformin is excreted both by the kidneys and the liver, and it was clearly necessary to refrain from treating diabetes with this drug when even slight impairment of kidney or liver function is present. There have, in fact, been many cases of metformin-induced lactic acidosis reported, though far less than have been seen with phenformin or buphormin, but all had acute or chronic renal disease[15]. There was, in fact, one author who maintained that phenformin-induced lactic acidosis was nothing to do with the biguanide, but some purely incidental event during the natural course of diabetes[16]. However, that this was almost certainly incorrect was established by our finding[15] that in 24 of the 34 relevant case reports in the literature at that time, the onset was within two months of starting the drug, and in 17 cases was within two weeks. Such an early concentration of onset of the condition would have been extremely unlikely if it was an incidental event. Soon after we had reported these cases to the Committee on the Safety of Medicines (see above), phenformin and buformin (a congener favoured in many European countries) were withdrawn by the Committee from the list of prescribable medications. One of the studies contributing to the demise of phenformin was led by Margaret Rose, one of my lecturers[17], who also worked with my group on the effect of metabolic acidosis on intracellular pH and lactate metabolism[18]. She later married a psychiatrist, Geoffrey Lloyd, and I did occasionally wonder whether working in my laboratory had resulted in her association with a psychiatrist!

Shortly after these cases occurred, I was due to describe them at a meeting of the Medical Pilgrims which happened to be taking place at The London. My presentation was the first on the agenda. A few minutes before the meeting started, I entered the lecture theatre and sat down in the third row, waiting to be called by the chairman. Just then, a little old man wearing an ancient sports jacket with leather patches over the holes in the sleeves at the elbows, came and sat down beside me. Now, simultaneously, in an adjacent theatre, there happened to be a meeting of the Hospital Porter's Union; in my youthful arrogance I assumed that this was a porter who had come to the wrong lecture theatre, and I was about to redirect him to the correct theatre, when I was called to give my paper. To my consternation, all through the following four papers, the 'porter' next to me whispered into my ear a series of the most devastating scientific comments on my paper. I thought that this was a highly peculiar sort of porter! Someone from the back of the theatre then got up and asked what Professor Krebs thought of my paper. To my horror, the 'porter' next to me rose and made a few polite remarks! Hans Adolf Krebs was a Nobel Laureate (1953) who had described both the tricarboxylic acid (TCA) cycle (which bears his name) and the urea cycle; both these cycles are fundamental to animal metabolism, the TCA cycle producing most of the energy for aerobic metabolism, and the urea cycle being the sequel of reactions by which most mammals dispose of unwanted nitrogenous waste products. I reflected that I had contemplated redirecting him to the Porters Union Meeting and prayed for the ground to open beneath me so that I could descend forever unto Avernus!

We then broke for the tea interval in the neighbouring Blizard Club, another room in the College where staff relaxed between giving lectures. Krebs came up to me with a dark, tall, dark and rather mysterious-looking character in tow, and said in his thick German accent

"Cohen I vood like you to meet my colleague, Frank Voods! You two vill write a book on ze subject of lactic acidosis, and I vill write ze preface!"

Frank Woods and I both clicked our heels together and said

    "Yessir!"

Krebs produced his preface, which was very long and discursive and embarrassingly, it seemed to suggest that Frank and I were the 'best things since sliced bread'! We eventually persuaded him to cut it down to a few lines. It took us three years to write the book[19], which eventually sold about 1600 copies. In it we defined two sorts of lactic acidosis, which we designated Type A and Type B. Type A is a commonplace accompaniment of conditions in which tissue perfusion is inadequate, due to, for instance, haemorrhagic shock or severe dehydration. It is due to the accumulation of lactic acid in the blood and tissues, because, owing to the lack of oxygen, it cannot be further metabolised to carbon dioxide and water. Type B is the variety in which there is no evidence, at least at the onset, of shock or poor tissue perfusion, as discussed already.

To return to Hans Krebs, he was born at Hildesheim, in 1900 and was the son of an ear, nose and throat surgeon of that city. He studied at the Universities of Gottingen, Freiburg-im-Breisgau, and also in Berlin, in the laboratory of Otto Warburg at the Kaiser Wilhelm Institute, who won a Nobel Prize for work on the biochemical mechanisms of *respiration. Warburg was nominated for a second prize for work on the mechanisms and enzymes involved in fermentation, and flavine, which is a component of flavine adenine dinucleotide, one of the components of the electron transfer chain involved in biological oxidations. In 1933 the Nazis terminated Krebs' appointment because he was a Jew, and he went to the laboratory of Frederick Gowland Hopkins, at the Cambridge School of Biochemistry. He then moved to Sheffield as a Lecturer, where he later became Professor and Director of the Medical Research Council's Unit for Research in Cell Metabolism. When this unit was later transferred to Oxford, he went with it and became Professor of Biochemistry at the University of Oxford. He once took me to see his personal archives, including the Nobel Prize citation. His papers and reminiscences[21] included a letter of rejection by *The Lancet* of his paper describing the Krebs Cycle! Some readers may be appalled at such a lack of insight by the Editor of the journal, but most medical scientists, myself included, will have had the experience of having what turned out to be a seminal paper rejected. The 'shock of the new' often seems to put reviewers off, many having been, no doubt, selected by the journal concerned to give a 'safe' opinion.

The universities of the UK and USA have, in a perverse way, much to be thankful for from the exodus of Jewish scientists fleeing Nazi Germany, including Albert Einstein, Fritz Haber, Leo Szilard, Max Planck, Max Perutz (who worked out the structure of the haemoglobin molecule), Werner Heisenberg (of Uncertainty Principle fame) and Max von Laue. This exodus is recorded in a volume by Jean Medawar and David Pyke (who was in my time the Registrar of The Royal College of Physicians of London)[22]. After Hitler's decree excluding all Jews from state institutions, about 1500 refugee scientists fled Germany, and organisations were set up in the UK and USA to receive them and get them university posts where they could continue their research. They helped turn the tide of war against the Axis Powers; however, it is interesting to reflect that the boot might have been on the other foot if they had to be allowed to stay in their home country.

Another example of German exiles of this sort is Wernher von Braun (1912-1977), the German-born rocket scientist, who designed the V2 rocket with which Hitler hoped to change the course of World War II. In his boyhood he played with rocket-propelled cars, and caused mayhem in a crowded street in Berlin by releasing a toy wagon propelled by firework rockets! In 1939 he was required to join the National Socialist Party, and it is believed that he was a mildly enthusiastic supporter of Hitler. He then became a member of the Allgemeine SS and regularly wore SS uniform. His feelings for Hitler's regime may have changed when he was arrested and accused of being a Communist sympathiser, who was attempting to sabotage the rocket development programme, which was being developed at Peenemünde, to which von Braun had been sent. Von Braun later admitted having used inmates of the Buchenwald concentration camp for menial jobs in his rocket laboratory. British intelligence got wind of this activity and heavily, but unsuccessfully, bombed the Peenemünde laboratories. Von Braun surrendered to the advancing Americans in 1945 and was transferred to the USA, where he worked on the nuclear ballistic missile programme. In 1957 the Soviet Union launch its unmanned satellite Sputnik, causing great jealousy in the USA. Von Braun was put to work on the development of the Saturn rockets for NASA, which eventually powered the successful Apollo 11 mission to land a man on the moon. He died of pancreatic and kidney cancer in 1977. Another émigré to the USA was Edward Teller (1908-2003), who became known as the 'father of the hydrogen bomb', though some of his colleagues thought that he had taken too much of the credit. He joined The Manhattan Project, which was concerned with the development of the H-bomb, and was a co-founder and later

Director of the Lawrence Livermore Laboratory. Numerous scientists of great distinction (e.g. Robert Oppenheimer, Arthur Compton, Enrico Fermi and Klaus Fuchs) were hosted by this organisation, set up at the time of the Cold War to counterbalance Soviet initiatives in the same field. Many of these individuals disagreed with each other over the ethics of what they were doing. At least one of them, Klaus Fuchs (1911-1988), was convicted of passing sensitive information to the Soviet Union.

One of Hans Krebs' Lecturers was Frank Woods, and this was, as described earlier, how I eventually came to meet Frank. Apart from our mutual research interests, Frank was a keen trout fisherman. I once went fishing with him near Sheffield. Frank's approach to this sport is quite the opposite of mine; whereas I move towards the river quietly and stealthily, he is extremely aggressive in his approach. I have often expected him to throw a hand grenade into the river and pick up the dead fish after the explosion – but as yet it has never quite come to this!

Another somewhat taxing patient I had was a 34 year old woman with a long medical history, the present episode consisting of right loin pain, which met the description of renal colic, such as I have described earlier in the case of my father. It was discovered during the course of investigation that the lady had a moderately raised level of plasma calcium. A common cause of this is a functioning tumour of one of the *parathyroid glands, but since the level of parathormone (the hormone secreted by these glands) was undetectable in her blood, it was clear that something was suppressing them. During our investigations the serum calcium rapidly rose to a level that was off the top of the scale of the machine used to estimate it and she began vomiting. So, eventually, we hit upon the ruse of sending her down to the X-ray department for further examination, and, in her absence, we took a look in her handbag (something we would not be allowed to do today) where we found 500 capsules of vitamin D (one of whose effects is to raise the plasma calcium), together with ampoules of calcium gluconate, the contents of which she had clearly been injecting into herself. These were removed and the calcium level fell to normal. Further enquiry revealed that since the age of fourteen she had attended no fewer than thirteen hospitals, with a variety of complaints, including pyrexia of unknown origin, *cystitis, and venous thrombosis and had undergone a surgical exploration of her abdomen because of unexplained abdominal pain. This is an example of Münchhausen Syndrome, a manifestation of a hysterical personality disorder. Baron

Münchausen (1720-1797) was a German nobleman who told many fantastic and impossible stories about himself. This name was applied to this pattern of self-harm by Richard Asher (1912-1969), a physician at Guy's Hospital. Asher wrote a number of important and somewhat unusual articles for medical journals. One of these was '*The Dangers of Going to Bed*[23], which described the complications of doctors keeping their patients in bed for too long. Another was '*The Seven Sins of Medicine*[24] which he listed as obscurity, cruelty, bad manners, over-specialisation, love of the rare, common stupidity and sloth. I have my own take on one or two of these. A good example of cruelty was commonly seen on ward rounds, when after the entourage, consisting of Consultant, Senior and Junior Registrars, House Physicians and Surgeons, and nurses had examined a patient they would retire to the end of the bed, get into a huddle and conduct a whispered conversation about the patient. This terrified patients, who often assumed that some dire condition had been discovered presaging an early and painful death! Another is over-specialisation; when I first started, every consultant physician was required to practise general medicine as well as their personal specialty. But, as time went on, there was an increasing tendency to abandon the general medicine and concentrate solely on one's particular specialty. This has had the effect of generating doctors of lower competence, because they have become less able to appreciate how the patient's condition interacted with others from which they might be suffering.

Since we were interested in the biochemical mechanism of *lactic *acidosis, we took the obvious approach of considering imbalances between lactate uptake and output. It was clearly important to look at the effect of externally imposed acidosis on the balance between lactate production and removal; because the main organ responsible for lactate removal is the liver, which largely uses it to fuel the production of new glucose (*gluconeogenesis), and this is where our attention was first focussed.

Someone who read '*Clinical and Metabolic Aspects of Lactic Acidosis*'[19] with some interest was Peter Stacpoole, Professor of Medicine, Biochemistry and Molecular Biology at the University of Florida, in Gainsville, Florida. He and I have been in contact over the years because he had developed a potentially useful adjunct in the treatment of lactic acidosis, namely sodium dichloroacetate (DCA). This substance increases the entry of pyruvate into the TCA cycle; it works by increasing the activity of pyruvate dehydrogenase (PDH), by inhibiting the kinase enzyme that normally phosphorylates PDH, thereby inactivating it and preventing the formation of acetyl coenzyme A, the point of entry into the Krebs cycle. One proposed use of DCA[25,26] was in the treatment of the acidosis of severe malaria caused by *Plasmodium falciparum*. Lactate levels are independent predictors of mortality in severe malaria, and the hypothesis was that reduction of lactate levels would reduce mortality. This idea was examined in a small number of West African children with the condition. The expected increase in the rate of fall of blood lactate was observed, and it was therefore necessary to proceed to a large scale clinical trial to test the hypothesis. This was all set up, but in the year that the trial was supposed to be done, the rains failed in West Africa. Since anopheline mosquitos, the vectors of *P. falciparum*, require rain to breed, there was little malaria and the trial had to be abandoned. To the best of my knowledge, the trial has not yet been done.

When I was visiting Peter Stacpoole in Gainsville, there was time for some diversionary activity. He arranged for me a boat trip down the Crystal River, the banks of which are lined with alligators resting their enormous jaws in the backs of large turtles in what appeared to be complete mutual amity. There were also a lot of baby alligators around and our boatman picked one up and invited me to stroke its belly. This looked exactly like an expensive lady's handbag, which it not surprising, for many of these female accessories are made of alligator or crocodile skin. Alligators may be found wandering around the streets in Gainsville and they sometimes get into one's garden, especially if it happens to back onto the river. I was required to give a talk on lactic acidosis after dinner in the University one evening, and was compelled to point out that after-dinner scientific talks are not favoured in the UK, since most audiences (the men, at least) are usually fast asleep by this stage of the proceedings. However, my audience were polite enough to maintain some semblance at least of listening to what I had to say.

Despite the fact that the DCA trial in the acidosis of severe *P. falciparum* malaria failed, we succeeded in doing some work on the pathogenesis of some of the complications of malaria, in cooperation with Michael English and his colleagues at the joint Kenya Medical Research Institute (KEMRI) at Kilifi, situated in the coastal plain bordering on the Indian Ocean. We found that the acidosis in these children was due in the first place to the accumulation of lactic and 3-hydroxybutyric acids.[27] The raised level of the latter was probably mainly due to inanition caused by the illness. The source of the lactic acidosis was somewhat more complex. Apart from the possible contribution of acidotic suppression of conversion of lactate into glucose by the liver, other possibilities included widespread blockage of tissue capillaries by the parasites and production of lactic acid by the parasites themselves. Finally, the haemoglobin-oxygen dissociation curve was shifted to the right, meaning that the red cells were less able to release oxygen to the tissues. This was partly due to a fall the concentration of *2,3-bisphosphoglycerate (BPG), a compound uniquely found in red cells; BPG binds to the haemoglobin molecule and decreases the latter's affinity for oxygen, thus promoting its release. BPG is synthesised in a side-reaction of the pathway from glucose to pyruvate and lactate; this synthesis is inhibited by acidosis, thus impairing oxygen release, and lactic acidosis is therefore promoted due to relative tissue *hypoxia. The significance of the accumulation of cases of malaria-associated lactic acidosis at sea level in Kilifi is related to the fact that that most of Kenya is on a plateau of height about 5000 feet. Since the relative of high altitude is a marked stimulus to BPG formation, those Kilifi children would have been partly protected against the tissue hypoxia of severe malaria had they been on the plateau, and, of course, part of the reason why Himalayan mountaineers take care to ascend over several weeks, camping out for a few days at each level, is to allow the full synthesis of extra BPG.

When I was still at work, one of the occasions I most looked forward to were the weekly meetings of what came to be known as The Metabolic Regulation Group, which took place every Friday evening in an extremely gloomy building that was part of University College London in Gower Street. The members of the group included Marion Spry (née Stubbs), Ian Mowbray and Richard Iles, amongst others. The meeting was preceded by the drinking of quantities of inferior wine, which the members funded by dropping a pound coin into a hat which was passed round. Members were expected to talk on their latest work, anything previously published being strictly forbidden. No sooner had the speaker of the day opened his mouth than he or she was interrupted by someone in the audience challenging what had been said. This sort of thing went on for about an hour, after which we all repaired to some local restaurant to soak up the alcohol with a decent meal. This was an excellent way of trying out one's latest material before a critical audience before submitting it to a journal for publication (after further stringent review by the journal's referees). On the wall of the University College corridor was a quotation from Thomas Sprat's 1667 '*History of the Royal Society*', parts of which I quote below:-

"It is strange that we are not able to inculcate into the minds of many men, the necessity of that *distinction* of my Lord Bacon's that there ought to be *Experiments of Light* as well as of *Fruit*. It is their usual Word, What solid good will come from thence? They are indeed to be commended for being so severe *Exactors of goodness*. But they are to know, that in so large, and so various an *Art* as this of *Experiments*, there are many degrees of Usefulness, without much delight: some may serve for real and plain *benefit*: some for *teaching*, without apparent *profit*: some for *light* now, and for *use* hereafter: some only for *ornament* and *curiosity*. If they will persist in contemning all *Experiments*, except those which bring with them immediate *gain*, and a present *harvest*; they may as well cavil at the Providence of God, that he has not made all the seasons of the year, to be times of *mowing, reaping* and *vintage*."

This is a pretty good defence of doing basic science. Now, I had many callow young Lecturers who demanded to be given some project that would immediately cure cancer, or eliminate ischaemic heart disease, whereas what was really needed was for some basic science groundwork to be done. So I showed them the above quotation and suggested that they should recite it to me 500 times, – to get the general idea into their immature brains. There is another passage along the same lines, quoted in a review by IF Skidmore of Hans Krebs' *'Reminiscences and Reflections*[21]:

"Even though some of your experiments may not bring fruition straight away, I hope they will be carried out immediately. This reminds us of what the great French Marshal Lyautey once said to his gardener:

"Plant a tree tomorrow"
The gardener replied:
"It won't bear fruit for a hundred years"
In that case, said Lyautey:-
"Plant it this afternoon""

Thomas Sprat (1635-1713), the author of the piece quoted above, was educated at Wadham College, Oxford, where he later was elected a Fellow. He took holy orders and became a prebendary of Lincoln Cathedral in 1660. He wrote his *'History of the Royal Society'* in 1667 and in 1684 became Bishop of Rochester. He was falsely accused of a plot to depose King James II, on the basis of a document found under a flowerpot in his manor, one of the conspirators having forged Sprat's signature.

Since I was the Medical College's alleged expert on acid-base regulation I had to consider many types of acid-base disturbance as well as lactic acidosis. One of these was ketoacidosis, in which the offending substances are 3-hydroxybutyric and acetoacetic acids. This condition is a common and very dangerous complication of poorly controlled Type I diabetes or incidental illness in patients with that condition. Ketoacidosis is often accompanied by a greater or lesser degree of lactic acidosis. This was generally attributable to the circulatory insufficiency and shock due to the vomiting and intense diuresis seen in ketoacidotic patients with diabetes. But it was also theoretically possible that inhibition of lactate entry into liver (the main organ of lactate disposal) was caused by the presence of the ketoacids. We found that 3-hydroxybutyrate and lactate inhibited each other's binding to preparations of liver cell membranes, thus substantiating the above suggestion. So it may be that lactate accumulation in patients with diabetic ketoacidosis is due, in part, to the inhibition of lactate transport into liver cells[28]. We also published a paper[29] on lactate binding to cell membranes, inferring that lactate was bound to some receptor in liver cell membranes as part of its entry process. Unfortunately we had later to publish a rather embarrassing retraction of part of this work, because we found that the laboratory plastic 'squirt' bottles of distilled water used in part of the study had a bacterial growth in them, and what we had been actually measuring was binding to bacterial cell membranes.

To remind the reader of the microstructure of the liver so that I can continue, it is comprised of closely packed lobules, of varying size, but in general they average about 0.8mm in diameter. The lobules consist of closely packed radial strings of hepatocytes; these strings extend from the extreme periphery of the lobule to the central venule. Blood is supplied by the hepatic portal vein (draining the intestine and spleen), and the hepatic artery, a branch of the aorta, and passes from the periphery of the lobule to the central venule through channels known as sinusoids, and thence to the hepatic veins and inferior vena cava (see Plate 6). The hepatocytes vary in their functions according to their distance down the radius of the lobule from the portal tracts, which are the spaces between the closely packed lobules. The technique of determining these functions was developed by Quistorff and his colleagues in Denmark, who perfused liver preparations with a solution of digitonin. This substance combines with the cholesterol of the cell membranes of the hepatocytes, causing destruction of the cell membrane so that the contents of the hepatocyte spill out into the perfusing solution. Quistorff perfused firstly in forward (antegrade) direction, destroying the peripheral zone of the lobule, and then studied the function of the central zone by preparing isolated hepatocytes from it, which remained viable. He then perfused digitonin in the opposite direction, and was able to study the hepatocytes from the peripheral zone in the same way. We thought we could develop this technique in two ways. Firstly, instead of isolating hepatocytes from the liver that remained viable after digitonin, we simply continued perfusing the liver with digitonin-free saline solution, containing sodium lactate as a substrate, because we felt that the study of the function of isolated hepatocytes was likely to produce results differing from hepatocytes *in situ*, because all sides of the hepatocytes were exposed in isolated cell preparations, whereas in perfused livers only the side of the cell facing the lumen of the sinusoid was available to the substrate. Secondly, we restricted ourselves to retrograde digitonin perfusion, since it was possible that in antegrade perfusion the products of cell destruction of lobules might have some unwanted effect on the more central cells as they flowed past. Thirdly, because the liver remained perfused after the digitonin perfusion, one could vary the time of digitonin perfusion, thus producing a range of degrees of destruction in a single perfused liver. In one study we compared the distribution of function in the lobules of rats rendered ketoacidotic by the administration of the specific pancreatic islet β-cell poison, streptozotocin (so that the islets could not synthesize insulin). This whole experiment was done, including the perfusion, inside the bore of a magnetic resonance spectrometer, so that intracellular pH could be measured. In the case of the perfusion of the ketoacidotic animals, the perfusate pH was kept at 6.8 to mimic the acidotic environment *in vivo*. The problem being investigated in this study was the apparent anomaly that formation of new glucose (gluconeogenesis) was known to be greatly increased in diabetic ketoacidosis (DKA), thereby accounting for the high level of blood glucose, despite the fact that in normal, non-diabetic, animals gluconeogenesis was well-known to be inhibited by acidosis, induced, for example, by the infusion of dilute hydrochloric acid or the oral administration of ammonium chloride. In normal animals, the pH in the periportal cells is markedly elevated compared with that in more centrally placed cells.

The situation was reversed in ketoacidotic animals. Normally, gluconeogenesis is maximal at the periportal end of each string of hepatocytes, but the situation is reversed in DKA.[30] The explanation we proposed was that in DKA the increased partial oxidation of fatty acids to acetoacetate and ß-hydroxybutyrate acidified the periportal cells, thus depressing their ability to perform gluconeogenesis. When those

1) The Matterhorn.
RDC (watercolour)

2) Portrait of Barbara by RDC.
(watercolour and gouache)

3) Wet weather in Bruges.
(RDC, oil)

4) Oil painting of Teignmouth, by Thomas
Luny.
(1759-1837)

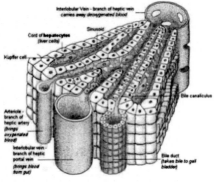

5) Boating at sunset, Redang, Malaysia.
RDC (watercolour)

6) The liver lobule (see text, page 93)

7) Ryolite rocks, Iceland, RDC. (watercolour)

8) Gateway to India, Mumbai

9) Cass Sculpture Park, Goodwood Statues by Anthony Gormley

10) Two tiles purchased in Lisbon. Left – a cockerel, national symbol of Portugal. Right – Bélem Tower, in River Tagus, Lisbon

11) Our house, 2013, Longmeadow. (East Dean, Chichester)

12) Barbara's 80th birthday party. Clockwise:- Sam, Barbara, Teresa, Tom, Steven, David and Susan Legg

13) Spinalonga, Crete. Entrance to Old Leper colony. RDC (watercolour and gouache)

14) Henningsvaer, Lofoten Islands, Norway. The buildings on the right are for storing cod. RDC (watercolour and gouache)

15) Water colours by Espolin Johnson – google.co.uk/imges

16) Spandrels, St Petersburg

17) Rat Liver with UCP2
stained as dark Brown
granules
C = centrilobular zone
P = periportal zone

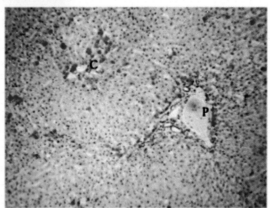

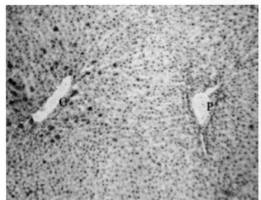

18) Rat liver similarly stained
for TRPv4
C = centrilobular zone
P = periportal zone

19) 'Health & Safety'
in Montenegro

acid ions are metabolised to carbon dioxide and water, they consume hydrogen ions in the process, and since in DKA this process takes place in the centrilobular cells, these cells are alkalinised, i.e. their internal pH rises. It is this that allows gluconeogenesis from lactate to proceed. I have described this project in some detail to illustrate the rather complex technical arrangements needed to solve problems of this sort.

Since we were interested in the biochemical mechanisms that produce lactic acidosis, we took the obvious approach of considering imbalances between lactate uptake and output. It was clearly important to look at the effect of externally imposed acidosis on the balance between lactate production and removal, and because the main organ responsible for lactate removal is the liver, where such removal is mainly effected during the reactions leading to new glucose production (*gluconeogenesis), it was to this organ that our attention was first focussed. We were impressed by the fulminating course of development of biguanide-induced lactic acidosis (the biguanide then commonly used in the UK was phenformin, and on the mainland of Europe it tended to be buformin) and we suggested that a vicious circle had been set up, illustrated in the following diagram:

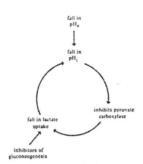

In this scheme, a fall in pH_e results in a fall in pH_i and inhibition of gluconeogenesis. This results in a decline of lactate uptake, initiating the vicious circle. A key reason for this development is that the rate-limiting enzyme of gluconeogenesis, *pyruvate carboxylase, is strongly pH-dependent. This is because *acetyl coenzyme A is an obligatory activator of pyruvate carboxylase (which converts pyruvate into oxaloacetate, the first intermediate in the gluconeogenic pathway *per se*), and this activation is markedly pH-dependent.

One of the conundrums we resolved at about this time was the fact that gluconeogenesis is actually greatly stimulated in diabetic ketoacidosis (thus leading to hyperglycaemia), though we had shown earlier that gluconeogenesis was actually inhibited by imposed external acidosis, e.g. by administering dilute hydrochloric acid, or ammonium chloride. We demonstrated[31] that the hepatic intracellular pH failed to fall in diabetic ketoacidosis, unlike the situation we had found in other causes of acidosis. We thought that the likely explanation was that the proton (H+) – consuming consequences of the high rate of gluconeogenesis more than counteracted the proton-generating effects of the of the 'ketone bodies' (i.e. 3-hydroxybutyric and acetoacetic acids).

Another possible determinant of the rate of *gluconeogenesis from lactate is the ability of the lactate ion to cross through the liver cell membrane. Simple diffusion of the non-polar lactic acid was a possibility, but it was not clear whether such diffusion could be sufficiently rapid to account for the known rate of gluconeogenesis, or whether there was, in addition, a lactate transporter which 'gingered things up'. We were aware of the work of Andrew Halestrap in Bristol, who had discovered that α-cyano-3-hydroxycinnamate inhibited lactate entry, and that of some other monocarboxylic acids into *erythrocytes. We therefore examined the effect of the cyanocinnamate compound on lactate entry into isolated rat hepatocytes, and found that, as in erythrocytes, it did inhibit entry and this is strong evidence for a transporter[29], which was also suggested by the fact that the mechanism was *stereospecific for the L-stereoisomer, since the entry of the D-lactate was not inhibited. Interestingly, the transporter was also inhibited by one of the substances responsible for the syndrome of diabetic ketoacidosis, namely 3-hydroxybutyrate, which could be an additional factor increasing the blood lactate level in this dangerous complication of Type 1 diabetes. I actually went to visit Andrew Halestrap in his laboratory in the University of Bristol. He was pretty sceptical of the idea of medical doctors getting involved in this sort of research, assuming that, because they could only do it part time because of their clinical duties, they must only be second-rate scientists. However, he seemed to grudgingly tolerate me, albeit with some rather sardonic amusement!

We also showed[30] that the carrier-mediated component of lactate entry into isolated hepatocytes was increased in starved and diabetic rats. This observation could partly explain the increased rate of gluconeogenesis under these conditions. It should be noted that, in isolated cells, substrates have access to much more cell surface than when they are *in situ* in the radial strings of hepatocytes in the liver lobule. This adds to the likelihood that transporter activity is an important determinant of the rate of *gluconeogenesis and, therefore, to alkalinisation of the liver cell, as explained above. We then showed[28] that the inhibition of lactate hepatic uptake and removal by 3-hydroxybutyrate occurred within ten seconds of the addition of the inhibitor, and from this were able infer that the inhibition of lactate entry was effected at the plasma membrane and not on some subsequent stage of gluconeogenesis. One of the co-authors on this paper was John Monson, who at the time was a Lecturer on the Medical Unit. We were due to present the findings at a meeting in Padua. John and I and our laboratory biochemist at the time, Hilary Metcalfe, booked a train that was scheduled via Paris, where we had to change to a train which would take us to our final destination. When, however, we got to Paris, however, we found that the staff of SNCF (the French national rail service) had gone on strike, so we hired a car. John and I drove it to Padua, myself at a reasonable rate, but John at breakneck speed, whilst Hilary went to sleep on the back seat.

To my surprise we arrived at our hotel in one piece; I thought it looked rather grand: but it turned out when we got to reception that no rooms had been booked in our names. Then the penny dropped; the receptionist pointed out that there was a hotel of the same name in a small village about ten miles outside Padua. So we made our weary way in that direction, and when we arrived it was an awful dump, probably with a negative star rating. But we put up with it and were able to enjoy some of the sights of Padua. These included the Anatomy Theatre of the University, built in 1594. This is an inverted coned-shaped structure allowing the student a clear view of the dissection proceeding on the floor of the theatre. Amongst the well-known scholars who worked there were Eustachio (who described the Eustachian tube, leading from the inner ear to the pharynx), Fallopio (who described the Fallopian tube, conveying ova from the ovary to the uterus, Morgagni (1682-1771), considered the father of modern pathology and Vesalius (1514-1564). The last of these made enormous contributions to anatomy, but like all pre-Harveian medical scientists, got a lot of the elementary physiology wrong. With regard to anatomy, he showed that many of Galen's ideas were simply wrong; Vesalius discovered that Galen had done his work on Barbary apes, since human dissection had been banned in Rome. Galen had assumed that arteries carried the purest blood from the heart to higher organs such as the brain, whereas the venous blood, less pure, supplied the intestines. This theory demanded that the ventricles were interconnected by small holes. For 1400 years after Galen many workers claimed to have found these holes, but Vesalius declared that he could not find them. He therefore hypothesised that it 'distilled' through the interventricular septum. In 1543 he published a seven volume work *'De humanis corporis fabrica'*. He also disproved the idea, deriving from the Garden of Eden, that a man had one less rib than a woman, a view no doubt deriving from Genesis 2, 21-23, which describes how God caused a deep sleep to fall on Adam (was this the origin of anaesthesia?) and extracted a rib, from which he made a woman.

Another of the seminal discoveries I saw reported during my career was made by David Barker of the University of Southampton, whom I first met at a conference in Iceland. This was that a number of diseases of adults were due to events occurring either *in utero* or in early neonatal life[31]. The molecular basis of this appears to be largely that of *methylation of the DNA of part of the relevant genes, which has the effect of silencing those genes. Sometimes the phenomenon is mediated by *acetylation or deacetylation of histones, the protein frameworks around which DNA is wound (what has always mystified me is the fact that, during cell division by the process of mitosis, there is a phase of demethylation, followed by remethylation in exactly the same place; I have never seen an explanation of how this degree of fidelity is ensured). An example of fetal programming is that fetal malnutrition, as judged by low birthweight, was associated with the development of high blood pressure in adult life. Furthermore, blood concentrations of *fibrinogen, clotting factor VII, and fasting glucose levels (raised in diabetes) are partly determined by events in fetal life and infancy. Manipulation of the diet of infants may partly determine the level of enzymes concerned in the synthesis of cholesterol, and therefore the incidence of cardiovascular disease, including myocardial infarction. We showed that rats whose mothers had been fed a low protein diet whilst pregnant had diminished levels of the enzyme *glucokinase, which occurs only in the liver and pancreas, gut and brains of humans and most other vertebrates. In the liver, glucokinase is confined to the centrilobular zone of the hepatic lobule, where it takes up glucose (some of which has been formed in the periportal zone) and either stores it as glycogen or uses it to fuel metabolic reactions. The first reaction, whichever pathway is followed, is the formation of glucose 6-phosphate. We also showed[32] that animals whose dams had been fed a low protein diet whilst pregnant, showed markedly less hepatic glucokinase, and, therefore, allowed more glucose to escape into the general circulation via the hepatic veins. We thought that this could be a factor in the pathogenesis of Type 2 diabetes.

One day I was at a scientific meeting being held in The Royal Society of Medicine. During the coffee break I went to the loo and standing in the next stall to me was Sir David Innes-Williams, a noted paediatric urologist. He said to me

"Bob – would you like to see how the charitable sector works?"

I, of course said "Yes" and this is how I got on the Council of the Imperial Cancer Research Fund (ICRF) of which Innes-Williams was chairman. In due course I rose to be Chairman, and one of my tasks in my approximately nine years in post was to entertain various visiting American oncologists. Looking for somewhere to do this, I settled on The Athenaeum Club in Pall Mall, which was close to The Royal Society and the Royal College of Pathologists. I got someone to propose me and thus became a member. One of the most interesting features was in the dining room, in which, if you were eating on your own, you usually sat at the so-called Club Table: here you met bishops, Fellows of the Royal Society, well-known physicians, and a variety of business tycoons. There is fairly reasonable accommodation in the Club and Barbara and I have stayed there overnight quite often, especially when we have some meeting or function to go to early the following morning. About 150 yards further down Pall Mall is the Reform Club, which has always had a sort of friendly rivalry with the Athenaeum. The story goes that during the First World War the Foreign Secretary of the day, Sir Edward Grey, used to walk from the Foreign Office to his club (The Reform) for lunch. As he got older and perhaps his prostate gland began to trouble him, he used to drop into The Athenaeum on the way to relieve himself. The members of The Athenaeum took exception to be used as a public urinal, and commissioned the Head Porter to challenge him on the next occasion that this happened. The Head Porter therefore accosted Grey, saying

"Sir! Are you a member of this Club?"

Grey, who was a noted wit, replied

"Oh! is this a Club?"

These Clubs tend to be most frequented by the more elderly and retired members; I was first taken to The Athenaeum when I was a House Physician by a well-known but ageing pathologist, Charles Gray, and when we went to the enormous coffee room, I could hardly restrain myself from giggling, since in it were about ten elderly members, all having a post-prandial snore behind their copies of *The Times*! You can tell that the Club is really geared to the elderly, since the male loos have fitted in each stall those sloping pieces of glass whose function is to catch the drips at the end of *micturition. This tendency to dribble becomes increasingly worse as the prostate enlarges with age.

Another organisation which I joined at its foundation in 1998 was The Academy of Medical Sciences. I have a suspicion that its set up was a response by many physicians to the very small number of their colleagues who managed to get elected to the Fellowship of The Royal Society, the prime scientific body in the UK. Its formation was recommended by a panel chaired by Michael Atiyah, a past President of the Royal Society, and the Academy's first President was Peter Lachmann. Its current aims, apart the usual stuff, such as the promotion of excellence, include, *inter alia*, nurturing the next generation of medical researchers, and linking academia, industry and the NHS. However, its Fellowship has not yet, and probably never will, acquire the caché of that of The Royal Society, because of the requirement that its Fellows must have something to do with the Medical Sciences. It does, however, put on several good symposia every year, which I often go to. From 2008, it met in the premises of the Novartis Foundation; Novartis was originally the pharmaceutical company Ciba, which ran an academic arm, rather in the same way as the Wellcome Trust is the academic side of the Wellcome Foundation and their premises is now where the Academy is based.

When I first joined the Council of the ICRF, the Director was Sir Walter Bodmer, who had made his reputation by his work on the molecular biology of colon cancer. By the time he retired from this post, I had become Chairman of Council, and it was my job to find a new Director. I did not have to look very far, since one of the ICRF laboratories was run by Paul Nurse, who was already a Fellow of The Royal Society. Nevertheless, I thought I should consult someone who really knew about these things, and decided to go to Sir David Weatherall at Oxford for advice. David Weatherall was a man of few words, and when I mentioned Paul Nurse's name to him, he took a few puffs at his (empty) pipe and said

"Real Stockholm material, that!".

So I put Paul's name to Council, which accepted it with alacrity. In due course, Paul got his Nobel Prize and went to Stockholm to receive it, in company with Tim Hunt and an American, Lee Hartwell, who between the three of them had worked out how the mitotic cycle was controlled. This is important because the mitotic cycle is central to the process of cell division and, when it goes wrong, the controls normally determining the appropriate rate of cell division are destroyed and cancerous tumours may result.

There were two charitable organisations funding work on cancer at the time I joined the ICRF Council, namely the ICRF itself, which did all the research it funded in its laboratories in Lincoln's Inn Fields, and The Cancer Research Campaign (CRC), which used its charitable funds for projects over the whole UK, in effect acting as a grant-giving organisation, awarding grants in response to refereed high quality grant applications. There are advantages to both systems: the ICRF approach recruiting the best quality researchers from all over the world, whereas the CRC system unearthed bright ideas which emerged in grant applications from equally wide sources. Paul Nurse felt that the interests of cancer research would best be served by merging the two organisations. So a small committee was set up consisting of the CRC Chairman, Jock Worsley, the CRC Chief Executive Officer, Gordon McVie, Paul Nurse and myself; in due course, agreement was reached on the formation of a merged organisation, to be known as Cancer Research (UK). Jock Worsley and I thought that Cancer Research (UK) ought to have a Chairman other than one of ourselves, since this would ensure that neither of the two previous charities would have undue influence on the activities of the new charity. Since we could not immediately think of anyone suitable, we took the somewhat unusual step of advertising in the national press for a new Chairman. The response to the advertisement contained only one person who might be suitable, namely Baroness Hélène Hayman, who was duly interviewed and appointed. Lady Hayman was a Labour Member of Parliament from 1974-1979, became a Junior Minister at The Department of Health and Minister of State at the Ministry of Agriculture, Fisheries and Food. She was made a Life Peer in 1996. Besides her political life, she had been involved in numerous health issue and medical ethics committees. In 2006 she won the election for the newly created position of Lord Speaker of the House of Lords.

When I was Chairman at the ICRF, I was invited to one of the Queen's Garden parties held in the grounds at the rear of Buckingham Palace. On these occasions the guests were shepherded into small groups, which were visited in turn by Her Majesty and its members were introduced to her. She had done her homework well and was able to talk very much to the point with each group. A number of tents were set up in the garden, where tea and cakes were available. One tent contained the toilets, in which you were handed towels to dry your hands by powdered flunkeys whose real purpose was, I suspect, was to examine you closely before you left to make sure that you were 'properly dressed'!

Meanwhile, Paul Nurse accepted an appointment as director of the Rockefeller Laboratories in New York. After some years he returned to the UK as Director of the National Laboratory for Clinical Research in a new building just north of King's Cross Station, and President of The Royal Society.

I have referred earlier to the club known as The Medical Pilgrims. Shortly after giving a paper to them at The London Hospital, I was invited to become a member. This club holds an annual meeting, which for two years out of three is in the UK while the third meeting is held at some well-known Medical Centre overseas. In order get the overseas meetings set up, the Pilgrims invite overseas scientists to join them at their UK meetings. On one occasion, there was an overseas meeting in Barcelona, the capital city of the Spanish province of Catalonia, which has a distinctive culture and language of its own. The Pilgrims stayed at the Hotel Colon, which is on the sea front, and the lecture theatre provided for us by the Medical School was reached through an underpass. Barbara and I were walking one morning through the underpass when we were approached by a beggar woman and her daughter. The woman held out a tray of trinkets in the apparent hope that we would buy something. However, Barbara was a bit suspicious of what was going on and knocked the tray upwards, to reveal that the small daughter had my wallet in her hand, having delicately abstracted it from my coat pocket! The miscreants took fright and rushed off, dropping my wallet which I gratefully retrieved. They had obviously studied the crimes of the Artful Dodger in a Spanish translation of '*Oliver Twist*'! In fact, Barcelona and Rome are well-known as the joint pickpocketing capitals of Europe, and the local authorities display many notices cautioning you to beware of pickpockets.

As indicated above, the Medical Pilgrims always invited a few distinguished doctors from overseas to join them, with the obvious ulterior motive that, sooner or later, they would be invited to hold their meeting in their home country. One of the people invited was Eberhard ('Ebo') Nieschlag, the Professor of Endocrinology at Münster. So, in due course, The Pilgrims were invited to Münster, where we were entertained royally by him and his wife, Susan. We found that, apart from the excellent wine he produced from his own vineyard, he had a daughter who had the most magnificent soprano voice, and she sang for us in the local church.

With regard to Rome, I have mentioned earlier Jack Ledingham's Chief Technician, Cliff Browning. He and his wife Hazel were once on holiday in Rome and were standing on a street corner, when some youth passed by on a Lambretta and snatched Hazel's handbag. They went back to their hotel to lick their wounds, but when they got to their room they found that it had been ransacked, and various valuables were missing. The room keys had been in Hazel's handbag, and unfortunately, they had the room number attached, so the thieves made good use of the opportunity. John Ellis, the Dean of The London, was once in Rome with his wife Joan when a similar bag-snatching event occurred. Joan managed to keep hold of the bag and was dragged along the pavement for some way. But eventually the thieves let go, and John and Joan went back to the hotel to clean up her extensive abrasions.

One of the duties of medical academics is to attend international conferences, both to present their own work and to hear what else was going on in the same field. Our NHS colleagues were obviously a bit jealous of these junketings and coined a phrase to describe a group of academics. This was 'an absence of professors'! One of my 'absences' was to a conference in Iceland, a country which I found so magical that Barbara and I subsequently went there for a holiday. The country's airline, Icelandair, has its main base in Keflavik, a few miles west of the capital Reykjavik. Reykjavik is an attractive city, built around two lakes. The roofs of the houses are usually galvanised iron rather than tiles, and painted in attractive red and green shades. One of the dishes to which I was first introduced in Reykjavik was monkfish tails, which I found delicious and Barbara and I have often eaten them since. We once saw a monkfish in an aquarium – it must be one of the ugliest creatures on the planet! Outside the two main cities, the capital and Akureyri, the roads are often unmetalled and are mainly constructed from volcanic ash; they also pass through various fords, where the water is of varying depth. For this reason it is inadvisable to take your car to Iceland, because it has a good chance of being a total write-off by the end of your visit. The best way to travel is by coach; these have expert drivers who are used to the conditions. We did a round trip of the island and returned by crossing the central highlands. All around you are volcanoes, often active, whose glowing lava flows down to the sea, causing enormous clouds of steam. There are some extraordinary rock formations to be seen – Plate 7 is a watercolour I did of ryolite rocks, which are multi-coloured.

As our bus guide told us, the terrain in Iceland is anything between zero and twenty million years old. Another feature of Iceland is the midge! Our bus driver had his windscreen wipers on all the time to get rid of the midges, which rapidly accumulated and blocked his view. We passed by Lake Myvatyn, where the midge population is notoriously great, Myvatyn being the Icelandic for 'midge'. The only place where we have experienced a similar midge density is in Northern Scotland, where we learnt to wear transparent veils over our heads for protection. You can, in fact buy a lotion called 'Jungle', which, if you smear it on exposed parts of the skin, does seem to provide some defence. Through Iceland runs the Mid-Atlantic ridge, where the Eurasian tectonic plate and the North American plate meet. These two plates are slowly separating by about 2.5 cm per year. No doubt because of the thinness of the Earth's crust in this region, there are many geothermal manifestations in the form of geysirs. The most dramatic of these is Strokkur, which erupts every four to eight minutes into a cloud of boiling water with spray and steam rising up to 40 m high. It is necessary to stand well clear at the first signs of an eruption!

Iceland has numerous glaciers, which slowly move down to the sea. Here, great chunks break off and fall into the sea with a tremendous splash, and if you are near in even a medium sized boat, there is grave danger of getting swamped. One of the precipitants of such a disaster is the eruption of a volcano under the glacier. Amongst these concealed volcanoes, Hekla is possibly the best example. One of the remarkable features of the glacier edges is the sky-blue colour of the ice at this point. We once tried walking on a glacier, something I would not recommend, since you will probably fall down and break something, or fall to your death in a crevasse which has been hidden by snow. You can get a dramatic view of the aurora borealis on fine nights, especially from the north coast. You may also see gyrfalcons hunting; these magnificent birds are the national symbol of Iceland and have wingspans of up to 130 cm.

When we reached the south coast of Iceland we were given another (alleged) 'treat'. This was a taste of rotten shark, a great Icelandic delicacy, prepared in the following manner. First, you catch your shark. You then bury it on the beach for about two months, by which time it is thoroughly rotten. You then dig it up again and start eating the flesh. We found the taste and smell thoroughly disgusting. Unlike the Malaysian durian, which smells horrible but tastes delicious, rotten shark is positively foul. One of our Icelandic treats was bathing in a warm geothermal pool at midnight – nice whilst you are in it, but the temperature contrast when you emerge is almost unbearable. The Icelanders have to amuse themselves during the long dark nights, and they have an attractive repertoire of rather haunting folk songs, of which we have a few recordings. The final unique Icelandic phenomenon is the Icelandic pony, which in addition to the usual gaits of walking, trotting, cantering and galloping, has an extra variety known as the 'tolt'. Whereas during trotting on an ordinary horse, the rider has to 'post' up and down to get in time with the up-and-down motion of the horse, during the tolt the movement is perfectly smooth and you simply glide along in great comfort. The only downside of my ride on an Icelandic pony was that I had no riding boots and my legs became painfully chafed. I now understand why those cowboys you see in Westerns wear those great protective flaps on their trousers!

Iceland is almost devoid of trees; when I walked through their sole apology for a forest, I found I was looking down on the tops of the trees, since none of them was much more than a metre high! The vegetation in Iceland, such as it is, is dominated by angelica, probably more familiar to readers as a culinary ingredient. Our final adventure in Iceland was on a walk, during which it was necessary to cross a stream of glacier melt about twenty metres wide. Barbara and I got over this obstacle fairly easily, but there was an elderly man who was obviously in difficulties, and he finally became stuck in the middle and got thoroughly soaked. We went into the stream and hauled him out, and then noticed from his facial appearance that he was obviously suffering from severe *myxoedema (under-activity of the thyroid gland), of which some of the visible manifestations are thickening of the skin, slowness of movement and a tendency to develop *hypothermia, which slows the sufferer down even more, and may finally result in coma. We pulled off most of his wet clothes, lent him our coats, chafed his cold feet, and got him into the bus, where he finally came to life again and advised him to see his doctor when we got back to the UK. I usually enjoy painting watercolours when travelling, but one of the downsides of trying to paint watercolours *'en plein air'* in Iceland is that your paints tend to freeze rather than dry on the paper, creating rather undesirable effects!

One of the reasons we went to Iceland was that I had read *"Pêcheur d'Islande"* ('An Iceland Fisherman') by Pierre Loti. This is a haunting and tragic novel about the life of Breton Fishermen, whose lives were spent in the stormy seas off the coast of Iceland, where shoals of cod abound. Many of these fishermen were drowned there, and the novel describes their wives in Brittany desperately scanning the horizon for any sign of their loved ones returning. Literary critics of the time said that he had adapted the Impressionist techniques of contemporary painters, Monet in particular, to prose. Pierre Loti was the pseudonym of Julian Vaud (1850-1923), a French Naval captain, who had sailed to many parts of the world, and was a prolific author. In *"Les Désenchantées"* (The Unawakened) of 1906, he described the life of women in a Turkish harem, possibly in response to a hoax played upon him by three Turkish women. In 1900 he went to China as part of the international expedition to combat The Boxer Rebellion, an uprising by Chinese Nationalists and Christians against foreign diplomats. The latter took refuge in the Legation Quarter, and were besieged by The Boxers (members of 'The Righteous Harmony Society'). Chinese officials wished to control the spread of opium, and confiscated supplies of opium from British traders; the British Government objected to this seizure and sent a military force to deal with the situation. The war finished with the 1842 Treaty of Nanking, which, *inter alia*, ceded Hong Kong Island to the British. In the 1990's it was returned to China by no less than Margaret Thatcher; even she apparently realised that she could not dispatch a naval task force to retain it, as she did in the case of the Falklands War of 1982. I once visited Hong Kong during the course of my travels; my principal recollection was of Chinese cuisine, which may be summed up by 'If it moves, they'll eat it!' I was introduced to 'Snake's Bile', which, when mixed with rice wine, is used as an invigorating beverage and appetite stimulant. In traditional Chinese medicine it is used for whooping cough, rheumatism, high fever, infantile convulsions, hemiplegia, haemorrhoids, bleeding gums and skin infections. Needless to say, none of these treatments has, to the best of my knowledge, been tested by a randomised controlled trial! There is a portrait of Pierre Loti, painted by Henri ('Le Douanier') Rousseau in 1891.

My visit to Hong Kong was part of a round the world trip, the next port of call being Hawaii. The Hawaii group of islands is, of course, a well-known tourist trap, and is none the better for it. When you arrive you are greeted by a group of allegedly attractive girls wearing grass skirts, swaying their hips provocatively, and draping garlands of flowers around your neck, shouting *"Aloha, aloha"* ("Welcome,

welcome!"); the celebrated Waikiki Beach isn't up to much, either. I walked around the backs streets of Honolulu, which weree no better than the slums of many well-known cities. I then flew on to San Francisco, which is notoriously hilly, but quite attractive. When we were taxiing on the runway, in preparation for take-off on the next stage, the captain of the aircraft, said:

'There's something wrong with the starboard engine!"

and aborted the take-off. A mechanic emerged, took off the engine cowling, fiddled about with a screwdriver, and replaced the cowling. The pilot then said:

"Well, let's try again and see what happens!"

All the passengers had their hearts in their mouths, especially as, at the point of lift-off, there was the wreck of a burnt-out crashed plane to be seen out of the porthole. As you may infer, we actually got off successfully, and the stewardess served tots of brandy all round!

Another time when we were involved in administering emergency medical aid was closer to home, in the village of Swanley, Kent. We were driving along, minding our own business, when we came across a road accident. It appeared that a woman had been knocked off her bike by a passing car. An ambulance had arrived and its crew were virtually sitting on the poor woman in an attempt to immobilise her, because their training had emphasised that any road traffic accident victim could potentially have a spinal fracture, and if they were moved, this could seriously damage the spinal cord and result in paraplegia. Barbara rushed over to them, sized up the situation and yelled

"Get off her, you idiots. Can't you see she wants to stand up?"

The ambulance men were completely fazed by the attack from this virago, and meekly moved away, whereupon the woman, who had some minor injuries, arose, dusted herself down and then joined the ambulance men in the waiting vehicle.

One of the conferences I attended was in Prague. Czechoslovakia is among several central European countries with a turbulent history, being occupied at various times by Germans and Russians even in the last century. One of its most notable personalities was Jan Masaryk (1886-1948). He was Foreign Minister from 1940-1948) and was a member of the Czech Government-in-Exile, which was based in London. In March 1948, he was found dead, dressed in his pyjamas outside the Foreign Ministry. The communist government, installed by the Soviets, declared that he had committed suicide by jumping out of the window, but there was considerable scepticism regarding this explanation, someone commenting sardonically that he must have been such a tidy man that he shut the window after himself. An investigation after the 'Velvet Revolution' of 1989 concluded that it must have been murder, pointing to the evidence of nail marks on the window sill, and the smearings of faeces thereabouts. The Prague police investigated further in 2004 and concluded that Masaryk had been thrown out of the window, a conclusion corroborated by a Russian journalist whose mother knew the Russian intelligence officer who had personally 'defenestrated' him.

A rather traumatic episode occurred during a visit to Amalfi, on the west coast of Italy, a few miles south of the bay of Naples. We had just boarded a motor boat which was taking a few tourists like us to visit various nearby beauty spots. An elderly man who didn't look all that well was the last person to board. Unfortunately he missed his footing, and fell off the quay straight into my lap! This was pretty painful and I developed an enormous intramuscular haematoma in one of my thighs, which resulted in my limping around in great discomfort for about three weeks. When we arrived at the first port of call, we were shepherded into a coach to be taken to Ravello, situated at the top of a nearby cliff. On the way up the winding road, we noticed that this elderly guy, who was seated just in front of us, was pale and had fingernails that were deeply concave, a condition called koilonychia and seen in severe iron deficiency anaemia. He then told us he had coeliac disease but had become fed up with his gluten-free diet, which must have been why he was so pale. The cause of his falling was narrowed down by these observations to faintness from the anaemia and the heat, or alcoholic intoxication, as he had been seen visiting the wine shops during the trip! The latter was probably a major factor as, once we reached Ravello, whilst we and virtually all the other tourists started walking around the little town to admire its beauties, the elderly man vanished straight into the nearest '*albergo*'!

As the old saying goes "*See Venice and die!*" we duly visited that extraordinary city (my second time, since I had been there much earlier with Nick Tarsh). As everyone knows, Venice is gradually sinking into the Adriatic and the city is frequently flooded at high tide, despite the only slight tidal rise and fall in the Mediterranean, so it is advisable to take wellington boots on any trip to Venice. Across the lagoon at Venice is the glass-blowing centre of Murano, and we hired a motor boat to take us there. The children were astounded, (and we were merely disgusted!) to see lumps of faeces floating around in the lagoon! However, the bad taste was taken away by watching the extraordinary skills of the glass-blowers.

For many years we had hoped to visit India, but had been frustrated by floods, exacerbated by the coincidence of the monsoon with tsumanis. Even on the occasion when we finally made it, the cabin crews of the airline on which we were scheduled to travel to from Heathrow went on a sudden strike. There was a rush of frustrated passengers to the booking office to find alternative means of transport, and in the end we found seats on a Swissair flight. The reason why we were visiting India was the occasion of Ampi's and Dandy's fortieth wedding anniversary. They had spent their honeymoon in Mumbai, but had stayed in a rather inferior hotel, because they couldn't afford anything better at that time. The best in Mumbai was the Taj Mahal Palace Hotel and they were determined to return to Mumbai on this anniversary and stay in that hotel. They invited about fifty of their friends and colleagues, including ourselves, to a celebration party. From our hotel room there was an excellent view of the bay outside the harbour and you could see the great arch known as 'The Gateway to India' (Plate 8). This was a monument built during the British Raj to commemorate the visit of King George V and Queen Mary in 1911. It is located on the waterfront overlooking the Arabian Sea and had been used as a landing place for British Viceroys and other visiting dignitaries. Following the country's independence in 1948, The Gateway was the point where the last British troops to leave India departed. It had a bomb planted in it in 2003 by terrorists attacking The Taj Mahal Palace hotel, where their British foes frequently were garrisoned. There were a number of good eating places in the vicinity of the hotel, but the most memorable was a fish restaurant on the seashore. It was infested by stray cats, hoping for a morsel of fish, despite large notices in the restaurant warning diners against feeding the animals. Whilst we were in our hotel room in Mumbai, we saw a trawler in the bay, apparently having a bonfire of some of its rubbish; however, as the flames rose higher and higher, we realised that the ship was actually on fire, and this conclusion was confirmed by the appearances of several fireboats with water hoses. The fire was eventually extinguished, but the following day we saw the ship being towed away, no doubt to the breaker's yard.

One of our favourite holiday destinations is the Hebridean island of Mull, which Barbara regards as a microcosm of the rest of Scotland. She should know, since she spent much of her childhood in Scotland, because her father who was a distinguished and innovative water purification Chartered Civil Engineer at the firm of Glenfield and Kennedy, the headquarters of which was in Kilmarnock. One of the places where we stayed was Tiroran House, located on Loch Scridain. This rather luxurious hotel had some regular customers who always arrived by helicopters, which landed on the lawn in front of the hotel. Those who want some strenuous exercise can walk to a fossilised tree on one of the beaches, and to some extraordinary rock formations known as Carsaig Arches. Another of our destinations was Tobermory, the main town on the island. This had a waterfront about 300 yards long, lined by shops and restaurants whose facades were painted in bright reds, blues and oranges to ward off the general gloom of the Scottish weather. The town was flanked on one side by a promontory, on which was situated the Western Isles Hotel. This overlooked the bay, giving views of the ferries, run by Caledonian McBrayne, transporting visitors and their cars from the mainland ports of Oban and Lochaline. Oban is a city which I always try to avoid, since Barbara always wants to patronise a jeweller's shop on the sea front (The Gem Shop, which specialises in semi-precious stones mainly originating from local rocks – e.g. obsidian, topaz, Ionian marble and amethyst). Another interesting place was Dervaig, eight miles from Tobermory, along a tortuous road with hairpin bends. Dervaig has a church with an unusual spire, of a type only seen in a few other nearby villages, and an excellent fish restaurant. Dervaig had a tiny theatre, where we saw a *"Death and the Maiden"*, a play by Ariel Dorfman, obviously linked with Franz Schubert's String Quartet No. 14. The whole effect was pretty magical.

We then went to Ulva, an island off the west coast of Mull, readily accessible by ferry, on which there are no made-up roads. We walked to Starvation Point, from where the victims of the Highland Clearances of the eighteenth and nineteenth centuries, and the Potato Famine of the latter century, escaped for America and other destinations more welcoming. The residents of the Ulva villages were forcibly ejected from their crofts by rich landowners who wanted their land for sheep grazing. Ulva was the ancient home of the Clan Macquarrie, one chieftain, (Lachlan MacQuarrie) was Governor of New South Wales from 1809-1821, where he undertook many building projects using convict labour; this was readily available since Australia and Tasmania were used as penal colonies for offenders in the UK. He returned home, and when he died a mausoleum was set up for him at nearby Gruline. In due course, we visited one of the now-disused Tasmanian penal settlements with Barbara's long-standing friend, Dorothy Blackburn, who had emigrated some years previously to Latrobe in Tasmania. Life in Tasmania is a little restrictive and Dorothy had a plane which she piloted herself on frequent visits to the Australian mainland. We have in our library a copy of Marcus Clarke's 1874 historical novel "*For the Term of His Natural Life*", which is an account of the experiences of one Rufus Dawes, a young man transported for a murder he did not commit. During our trip we visited Sydney where we saw the memorial to Lachlan MacQuarrie. Walking in Tasmania with Dorothy, we saw some of the unique Tasmanian fauna, including the Tasmanian Devil, and the Spotted Quoll. We brought home with us a cuddly model of the latter which we still have in our kitchen.

Just off the coast of Ulva lie the Treshnish Islands, the largest of which is Bac Mor, also known as the Dutchman's Cap because of its unique shape, presumably because of its origin as a volcanic outcrop, with subsequent washing down of the soil into the sea. These are a few miles north-west of the Isle of Staffa, to which we took a boat trip. The cliffs of Staffa are composed of vertical basalt columns, some of which enclose the cavern known as Fingal's Cave where we were landed so that we could go inside. Of course, as we landed, some musical device in the boat played Mendelssohn's Fingal's Cave overture (how corny!). We later took a boat from Fionnphort in Mull to Iona, to visit the ancient monastery, founded by St. Columba (521-597AD) in 563AD. This monastery was the centre for the spread of Christianity in Scotland amongst the heathen Picts. St. Columba originated from Derry in Ireland, from where he emigrated to Ireland because of an apparently trivial dispute with Saint Finnian of Moville Abbey over his right to keep a copy of a psalter that he had copied. This eventually resulted in a pitched battle at Cul Dreimhne in 561AD. Because of the numerous deaths in these battles, he was threatened with excommunication, but eventually he was allowed to go into exile instead. On his death in 597AD he was buried in the monastery.

I must now say something about Scottish cuisine; top of the pops for me is the haggis, to which I am deeply addicted. Unlike what some would like to believe, the haggis is not a wild animal which has to be hunted. It is, in fact, a concoction of sheep's heart, liver and lungs (i.e. offal), mixed with onion, oatmeal, suet, spices and salt, all encased in a sheep's stomach. It is best simmered in boiling water for about three hours, and dollops of the contents ideally served with 'bashed neeps' (turnips) and tatties (mashed potato). It is best swilled down with a 'wee dram' (a tot of whisky). It's certainly a way of getting rid of a lot of stuff which might normally go straight into the dustbin! This dish is one of the most notable contributions to global cuisine. It was seized upon by Edward Lear in one of his nonsense poems featuring Dr. and Mrs Haggis-on-Whey; I suspect this may be lampoon on Hay-on-Wye, which is the great UK second-hand book centre, where you buy books not by their individual prices, but by the kilogram! Finally, if you look up Scotland on Wikipedia you will find one entry described as 'a shithole country to the north of England, full of haggis-eating, caber-tossing alcoholics'.

When I was a final year student at The London Hospital there were two new appointments to the staff, Willie Irvine and David Ritchie. Willie was a rather short man, and, when I later became his house surgeon, one of my duties was to place an orange box by the side of the operating table for him to stand on! Willie used to cover the roller blackboard of the lecture theatre with facts, and before the poor students had time to write them down he switched to the other side of the blackboard to inscribe yet more facts. We were getting a bit fed up with this so on one occasion, when he pulled the roller board to get to the other blank side, he found that someone had written in enormous letters 'Remember Glencoe!' Willie was always rushing off to other hospitals to watch exponents of new operations so that he could later perform them at The London. Being a small surgeon, he specialised in very big operations such as hind-quarter amputations; at the end of the operation I was often in some quandary as to which piece to send back to the ward and which to send to the pathology department! David Ritchie was somewhat less manic, and after I had performed some small personal medical service for him when I was his House Surgeon, presented me with a very high quality split cane fishing rod. This resulted in my learning how to fish for trout.

In 1968 The London Hospital joined the Department of Health and Social security's experimental Real-Time Computer Programme. Computers had previously been used in hospitals in the USA, but this was almost exclusively to send bills for services rendered to individual patients. This was, of course, unnecessary in the UK, since National Health Service costs were funded by part of the Income Tax levied by the Government of the day. This gave The London Hospital the chance of developing more clinically relevant applications, and the Hospital's management therefore set up a group to consider what should be tackled. This group consisted of the Chief Executive (Michael Fairey) his deputy (David Kenny), the Head of the department responsible for paying salaries and bills (William 'Bud' Abbott), a senior chain-smoking nurse (Maureen Scholes), the Head of the Operational Research department (Barry Barber) and myself. This group met every Tuesday afternoon in the Computer Department to plan operations. Bud ran his financial operation using a very early British Computer, the Elliott 803, which used punched paper tape as its method of inputting data. This was very slow, and the paper tape was liable to jam or tear in the reading device. The computer was housed in the basement of the Resident's Hostel, and on one occasion was inundated by the contents of a barrel of beer which had been overturned in a wild party on the floor above. Furthermore, its entrance was immediately adjacent to the Venereal Disease Departments, whose clients were furtively trying to find the entrance to the VD clinic, and often wandered into the computer room itself. The whole group of us were commissioned to find out which was the best computer with which to replace the old 803 and were sent on trips abroad to help chose the successor. We eventually alighted on Univac, a firm whose headquarters was in Sweden (mind you, Univac had provided us with the most lavish entertainment of all the computers companies!). Their machine would support terminals in the form of visual display units in all the wards and administrative offices. The first application we developed was the Clinical Laboratory System, which allowed doctors on the wards to both make requests for tests and view their results from the ward, rather than wait many hours – or sometimes days – before the results slip was delivered, or, alternatively, making a visit to the laboratories to try to extract the result from one of the technicians. An additional refinement followed the development of apparatus which would make up to twelve tests (the Autoanalyser); our computer technicians connected the output of this machine directly to the ward terminals. For a short time The London Hospital Computer System[33,34] was a sort of Eighth Wonder of the World, and people came from far and wide to see it. One of the main sources of resistance to its installation were a group of our hospital consultants, so we arranged a series of whole day sessions for them in the Computer Centre, in which we explained the workings of the system and gave them good food and wine. By the end of the day these consultants believed they had invented the system themselves, recommended it to other consultants and complained loudly on the rare occasions when the system went 'down'. Since at that time the installation and running of computers systems was very expensive, management required that they should be evaluated for cost-effectiveness. I gave a paper on this topic, in so far as the evaluation effort in the UK was concerned, at a 1979 computer conference in Berlin[24]. Lastly, but most importantly, after a few years of these Tuesday afternoon meetings we actually managed to wean Maureen off the cigarettes!

An important event during my last few years before retirement was an investigation into the organisation of London Hospitals and Medical Schools[35], chaired by Sir Bernard Tomlinson, a pathologist from Newcastle, i.e. pretty far away from London, and he was therefore quite dispassionate. There were twelve of these Hospital and Medical School set-ups, and it had begun to be thought that this was rather inefficient, since all the specialties had to be repeated in each set-up, and research was impeded by the lack of what was called 'critical mass'. There were also lot of small specialist hospitals, e.g. Moorfields Eye Hospital, the Hospital for Tropical Diseases, which suffered from the same problems of small size and overspecialisation. This meant that the organisations were so small that cross-fertilization of ideas between different staff and disciplines were not too likely to occur. By far the most important recommendation was that the components of the organisations should be combined together in various ways. Thus University College and the Middlesex Hospital Schools were to be combined, as were St. Thomas's and Guy's, and, *horrible dictu*, Bart's and The London. Bart's didn't appear to think much of The London, which was thought to operate in some sort of slum in the East End, and The London Hospital and its Medical College thought that Bart's was too near to the City of London, and the rich tycoons therein, which formed a large part of the Bart's clientele, had nothing like the variety of interesting pathology that The London had. It was indeed true that The London benefitted from the fact that immigrants seeking asylum in the UK very often settled at first in the East End, with their great variety of tropical diseases, e.g. malaria, *leishmaniasis *oncocerchiasis and leprosy. My counterpart at Bart's was Michael Besser, Professor of Medicine and Endocrinology, who fiercely defended Bart's independence and didn't think much of the idea of merging with slum doctors – perhaps they might put off the City gentlemen! There was also the problem, common to all merging organisations, of who should be the boss, i.e. who should be the Professor of this or that – the Bart's man or the London man (or woman). However, these seemingly intractable problems were solved in one way or another and the merger proceeded in a state of rather suspicious armistice. After we retired, we got to know the Besser's quite well, and visited each other in our homes in East Dean and Climping, the latter being a pretty draughty village in the Arun district of Sussex, very near the seashore. Valerie Besser was a High Court judge and rather scared the wits out of me, but was very good company. Further interesting company was found in the nearby Cass Sculpture Park, although it was mostly made in metal (Plate 9).

Two countries that we had never previously visited together were Spain and Portugal, so we decided to rectify this omission in 2008. We flew to Bilbao, where our hotel was right opposite the Guggenheim Museum, designed by Frank Gehry, an outstanding piece of modern architecture, as opposed to its contents, which we did not find particularly interesting. Frank Gehry was born in 1929 in Toronto; his father was Ephraim Goldberg, who changed his surname to Gehry when the family moved to Los Angeles in 1947. His work attracted international attention after he designed a library in Hollywood, the California Aerospace Museum, and the Loyola University Law School. On the entrance slope to the Guggenheim is a topiary statue of a 40 feet high puppy dog, designed by Jeff Koons (1945-), made of marigolds, begonias, impatiens ('Busy Lizzie'), petunias and lobelias. (We understand that the Bilbao locals refer to the Guggenheim as 'the dog kennel'). Koons was a fan of Salvador Dali, which may explain some of his work! Also in Bilbao is the Bilbao Fine Arts Museum, which is situated in very attractive gardens and has, *inter alia*, a fine collection of the paintings of Jesús Maria Lazkano, who specialised in depicting architecture. His paintings include depictions of the ruins of Imperial Rome, the New York skyline and buildings by Mies van der Rohe and Frank Lloyd Wright; they have a certain surrealist element, derived from Caspar David Friedrich and possibly Salvador Dali, though he never goes nearly as far as the crazy paintings of the latter (*vide infra*).

We then hired a car and started driving along the north coast of Spain, passing through Santander and Gijón, before turning south, through Oviedo. This route is followed by those on a pilgrimage walking to Santiago de Compostela, the capital of Galicia. The object of the pilgrimage is to pray at the shrine of St. James the Great, a shepherd who whilst watching his sheep at night was, according to medieval legend, guided by a bright star. Though we did not go to Santiago, my brother-in-law, David Jarvis, did, My sister Ba followed him by car so that she could pick him up if he developed blisters! We also first visited Burgos, in whose cathedral the national Spanish hero, Rodriguez Diaz de Viva ('El Cid' (1043-1099)), is buried. According to legend, when he died, in order not to demoralise the Spanish troops who were fighting the Moorish invaders, his corpse was dressed in his armour, and he was put on his horse Babieca, and then apparently led his knights to victory at the battle of

Valencia in 1099. His armour was necessary to keep him in the upright position, but, no doubt, *rigor mortis* also helped! Needless to say, El Cid was the subject of an epic film of that name, starring, of course, Charlton Heston (of Ben Hur fame) and Sophia Loren.

We then crossed into Portugal near Braganza, which is also the name also of a noble house into which Catherine of Braganza (1638-1705) was born. She became the wife of King Charles II of England. She was unpopular because she was a Catholic at the time when the Protestantism of Martin Luther was spreading rapidly in England. She was accused of the 'Popish Plot', a plan to poison the King and to restore Catholicism. Although she was meant to stand trial for high treason, the King pardoned her, despite his bevy of mistresses. Catherine is credited with introducing the custom of drinking tea in Britain, and, for this, millions in this country (and, no doubt, in India, Ceylon and China) must owe her a debt of gratitude.

On this visit to Spain, we drove over the River Douro, the site of Wellington's campaigns in the Peninsular War (1808-1814). Wellington, when he was not known to his troops as 'Old Hookie' (because of the aquiline shape of his nose) was nicknamed 'Old Douro'. After sampling these reminders of the history of this nation, we moved on to Lisbon. The things which most stick in my memory about Lisbon are the Bélem Tower (Plate 10), on a small island in the River Tagus and the village of Sintra. The latter is on a cliff to the north of Lisbon and one of its main attractions is the Pena National Palace, the architecture of which is an expression of 19th century Romanticism. It has a very long history; the original building, which functioned as a monastery, was destroyed by an earthquake, being rebuilt by Ferdinand II between 1842 and 1854. It is now used by the Portuguese Government for State occasions, is open to the public and was well worth visiting. It has a motley mixture of architectural styles, including Moorish, Neo-Gothic and Neo-Renaissance. It stands in a large park, with many trees imported from abroad, including tree ferns from as far away as New Zealand. Finally, Portugal is renowned for producing beautiful glazed tiles, so we purchased a few of these with which to decorate various rooms at home. One of these shows the Bélem Tower, another depicts a cockerel, the national symbol of Portugal (see Plate 10).

References

1) Blake,W. *The Tiger*. Songs of Experience (1974)

2) Mazza M, Capuana A, Bria P and Mazza S. Ginkgo biloba and donezepil: a comparison in the treatment of Alzheimer's dementia in a randomized double-blind study. *European Journal of Neurology* 13, 981-985, 2006

3) Schneider LS. Ginkgo and AD: key negatives and lessons from GuidAge. *Lancet Neurology* 11, 851-859, 2012

4) Barnett D, Cohen RD, Tassopoulos CN, Turtle JR, Dimitriadou A and Fraser TR. A method for the estimation of Krebs cycle and related intermediates in animal tissues by gas chromatography. *Analytical Biochemistry*, 26, 68-84, 1968

5) Robb-Smith AHT. Thallium and a pale horse. *Lancet ii*, 872, 1987

6) Ledingham JM and Cohen RD. The role of the heart in the pathogenesis of renal hypertension. *Lancet* ii, 979- 981, 1963

7) White RW, Cohen RD, Vince FP, Williams G, Blandy J and Tresidder GC. Minerals in the urine of stone-formers and their spouses. In: *Renal stone research symposium*. Eds. Hodgkinson A and Nordin BEC. J & A Churchill Ltd, London 1968, pp. 289-296

8) Cohen, RD. Water and electrolyte metabolism during the treatment of myxoedema. *Clinical Science* 25, 293-303, 1963

9) Cohen RD. *MD Thesis*, 1966

10) Waddell WJ and Butler TC. Calculation of intracellular pH from the distribution of 5,5-dimethyloxazolidine-2,4-dione (DMO). Application to skeletal muscle of the dog. *Journal of Clinical Investigation,* 38, 720-729, 1959

11) Savege TM, Ward JD, Simpson BR and Cohen RD. Treatment of severe salicylate poisoning by forced alkaline diuresis. *British Medical Journal* 1, 35-36, 1969

12) Henderson RM, Bell PB, Cohen RD. Browning C and Iles RA. Measurement of intracellular pH with microelectrodes in the rat kidney in vivo. *American Journal of Physiology* 250, F203-F209, 1986

13) Andrew, ER, Bydder, G, Griffiths, J, Iles, RA and Styles, P. *Clinical magnetic resonance imaging and spectroscopy*. John Wiley and Sons, Chichester, 1990

14) (a) Cohen RD, Ward JD, Brain AJS, Murray CR, Savege TM and Iles RA. The relation between phenformin therapy and lactic acidosis. *Diabetologia* 9, 43-46, 1973 and (b) Cohen RD. The relative risks of different biguanides in the causation of lactic acidosis. In: *Research and Clinical Forums* 1. 125-134, 1979

15) Roche C, Nau A, Peytel E, Moalic JL and Oliver M. Severe lactic acidosis due to metformin: report of 3 cases. *Annals Biologique et Clinique* 69, 705 711, 2011

16) Sadow HS. This question of lactic acidosis. *Postgraduate Medical Journal* 45, May Supplement, 1969, pp.30-35

17) Lloyd MH, Iles RA, Walton B, Hamilton CA and Cohen RD. Effect of phenformin on gluconeogenesis from lactate and intracellular pH in the isolated perfused guinea pig liver. *Diabetes* 24, 618-624, 1975

18) Lloyd MH, Iles RA, Simpson BR, Strunin JM and Cohen RD. The effect of simulated metabolic acidosis on intracellular pH and lactate metabolism in the isolated perfused rat liver. *Clinical Science and Molecular Medicine* 45, 543-549, 1973

19) Cohen, RD and Woods HF. *Clinical and Biochemical Aspects of Lactic Acidosis.* Blackwell Scientific Publications, Oxford, 1976

20) Krebs HA. Rate control of the tricarboxylic cycle. *Advances in Enzyme Regulation* 8, 335-353. 1970

21) Krebs HA. *Reminiscences and Reflections.* Oxford University Press, 1981, pp. 298

22) Medawar J and Pyke DA. *Hitler's Gift.* Arcade Publishing, 200, pp. 268

23) Asher R. The Dangers of Going to Bed. *British Medical Journal* ii, 967-968,1947

24) Asher R. The Seven Sins of Medicine. *Lancet* ii, 358-349, 1949

25) Stacpoole PW and Felts JM. Diisopropylammonium dichlorate (DIPA) and sodium dichloroacetate (DCA): effect on glucose and fat metabolism in normal and diabetic tissue. *Metabolism.* 19, 71-78. 1970

26) Agbenyega T, Planche T, Bedu-Eddo G, Ansong D, Owusu-Ofori A, Bhattaram A, Nagaraja NV, Shroads AL, Henderson GN, Hutson AD, Derendorf H, Krishna S and Stacpoole PW. Population kinetics, efficacy, and safety of dichloroacetate for lactic acidosis due to severe malaria in children. *Journal of Clinical Pharmacology* 43, 386-396, 2003

27) Sasi P, Burns SP, Waruiru C, English M, Hobson CL, King CG, Mosobo M, Beech JS, Iles RA, Boucher BJ, Cohen RD. Am J Trop Med Hyg. Metabolic acidosis and other determinants of hemoglobin-oxygen dissociation in severe childhood Plasmodium falciparum malaria. *American Journal of Tropical Medicine and Hygiene,* . 77:256-60. 2007

28) Metcalfe HK, Monson JP, Welch SG and Cohen RD. Carrier-mediated efflux of ketone bodies in isolated rat hepatocytes. *Clinical Science* 71, 755-761, 1986

29) Monson JK, Smith JA, Cohen RD, and Iles RA. Evidence for a lactate transporter in the plasma membrane of the rat hepatocyte. *Clinical Science* 62, 441-420,1982

30) Burns SP, Cohen RD, Iles RA, Bailey RA, Desai M, Germain JP and Going TCH. Zonation of gluconeogenesis, ketogenesis and intracellular pH in livers from normal and diabetic ketoacidotic rats: evidence for intralobular redistribution of metabolic events in ketoacidosis. *Biochemical Journal* 343, 273-280, 1997

31) Barker DJP. *Fetal and Infant Origins of Adult Disease.* Ed. Barker DJP. Published by the British Medical Journal, 1992, pp. 343

32) Murphy HC, Regan G, Bogdarina IG, Clark SAJL, Iles RA, Cohen RD, Hitman GA, Berry CL, Coade Z, Petry CJ and Burns SP. Fetal programming of perivenous glucose uptake reveals a regulatory

mechanism governing hepatic glucose output during refeeding. *Diabetes* 52, 1326 -1332, 2003

33) Barber B, Cohen RD and Scholes M. A review of The London Hospital Computer System. *Medical Informatics* I, 61-72, 1976

34) Cohen RD. Evaluation of computer systems in Medicine. Proceedings of *'Medical Informatics Berlin 1979'* Eds. Barber B, Grémy F and Wagner G. pp. 931-937

35) Tomlinson, Bernard. *Report of the Inquiry into London's Health Service, Medical Education and Research.* Her Majesty's Stationery Office, 1992

Chapter 4

Retirement

The statutory retirement age in The Universities of London and Cambridge was sixty-five, or, more precisely, the end of the academic year of your sixty-fifth birthday. Barbara retired in winter, 1999, and I did so about nine months later. I had been looking forward to retirement for the previous two years because I was beginning to find the endless round of ward and emergency duties slightly tedious. But, of course, after I had retired I was pretty desperate for some sort of activity, preferably mind-taxing, other than walking the countryside and patronising the local restaurants. What I eventually did was finish a few scientific projects and papers which were already on the stocks, and write some monographs. The first thing to do was to find somewhere to live – we certainly were not going to stay in our London home in Beckenham for the rest of our lives. We had lived there for over thirty years, getting up at 7.00 a.m. and driving nine miles to work at The London Hospital, through horrendous traffic and then through the Rotherhithe Tunnel under the Thames. We were fed up with both the traffics fumes and the waste of time, it often taking over an hour to travel this short distance. Furthermore, since we were out all day, we had got to know virtually no-one locally except our next door neighbours, Jan (a Health Visitor) and Mike Parke (a Government lawyer). So, shortly before retirement, we decided to spend some time travelling across the south of England from east to west, looking for an attractive home in the country, since we had had our fill of town life. We also were anxious to be within reasonably close distance of our children and grandchildren. Susan, her husband David Legg, and their children Stephen, Philip and Harry lived in Ashford, Surrey. Martin, his wife Teresa and their children Samuel and Thomas had their home in Funtley, near to Portsmouth. Martin worked in Portsmouth for company designing and building radar satellite equipment for surveying the surface of the Earth. When we got to Chichester we saw in an estate agent's window a notice of a small cottage in East Dean, which was about seven miles north of the city in a fold of the South

Downs. This seemed ideal for a weekend cottage, but no good for living in permanently after retirement, because it was far too small to take our furniture, books, clothes, paintings and other domestic articles. So we bought the small cottage (Spring Cottage) in the village of East Dean and drove from Beckenham to East Dean every other weekend, with the intention of looking for something more permanent.

Just north of our house in East Dean is New House Lane, about a mile long (Plate 10). Halfway along it are the works of West and Son, which make very beautiful furniture, French-polished and often inlaid with elegant decorations, but very expensive, since a single piece may take up to six months to make. At the end of New House Lane is a farm which prides itself on its flock of Southdown sheep. The sheep of this breed have rather flat faces and very woolly coats; they remind me of the sheep painted by Samuel Palmer during his Shoreham period. When we lived in Beckenham in South East London, we often drove to Shoreham, in the valley of the River Darenth at weekends, where Palmer's old house had been turned into a small commemorative museum. Palmer (1805-1881) was much influenced by the mystical and visionary work of William Blake. By far his best work was produced when he lived at Shoreham, his subsequent work being somewhat mundane. The Ashmolean Museum in Oxford has a good collection of Palmer's work; not all of it is on display, but the curator, given notice, will dig it up out of the archives for you.

East Dean is about seven miles north of Chichester in West Sussex, which we visited when we couldn't stand much more of London suburbs. This fit of aversion seemed to come upon us regularly about once a fortnight! We rather liked East Dean and decided that it might be a good place to find a suitable house in which to spend our retirement – Spring Cottage was certainly far too small Just opposite Spring Cottage was a house (Longmeadow) which might be the right place. When we took possession of Longmeadow, our present home, it was not surprisingly in a dilapidated state, needing a lot of decoration, especially to remove the quantities of brown 'marmalade' paint adorning the various wooden surfaces. One of the front rooms had obviously been a bathroom of some sort, since it contained a hideous mauve-coloured wash basin. One great advantage was that it had three loos and two bathrooms, so queues do not develop when we have several guests. I am always reminded of this blissful state of affairs every time I use the gents' toilet in The Athenaeum Club, in which as you stand relieving yourself you can look at a cartoon depicting a queue of dogs with agonised looks on their faces waiting for their turn at a single lamp post!

We bought Longmeadow at the bottom of the housing market, and the previous owners kept on reducing the asking price to try to attract a customer. We were able to use much of what we had saved by buying at *le moment juste* and spent what we had thereby saved on much-needed redecoration. We eventually turned the room with the mauve basin into a library, for our approximately three thousand books, of which the most ancient and venerable are W Cheselden's '*The Anatomy of the Human Body* (1792) WH Prescott's *History of the Conquest of Mexico*[3] (1878) describing the shady doings of Hernan Cortés and his crew, GE Male's '*Juridical Medicine*' (1818), the first volume of '*The Works of Thomas Sydenham*' and the 1927 edition of *The Encyclopaedia Britannica*, (which I use mainly to help me complete the *Times 2* and *Independent* crosswords and code-words). I never attempt the cryptic crosswords of these broadsheets, since in my view they can only be completed by those whose minds are twisted in the same direction as that of the compiler. I also have almost a complete set of the works of my favourite author, Jane Austen, and an almost complete one of the works of Anthony Trollope, having much sympathy with that bishop (who shall remain nameless!) who in an unguarded moment said

"Whenever I am bored, I go to bed with a Trollope"!

I have found that the only thing which can keep me awake in trains was to do crosswords and code words, and *The Times* fortunately published a number of books of these puzzles, which I took around with me on long journeys, when, for reasons explained later, it was necessary to stay awake.

Longmeadow had a burglar alarm system and an internal alarm system, the business end of which was an array of klaxons in the greenhouse of the type used by fire engine crews to clear a way through traffic on their way to a fire (or a cat up a tree!). This alarm system could be set off to call for help either with a hand-held radio switch or by pressing a red button on wall-mounted consoles distributed about the house. These buttons are irresistible magnets for small children who happen to be visiting and a number of false alarms have therefore occurred. These items had been installed by the previous owner of the house, who was a manufacturer of spare parts for fire engines. If the alarms were set off, three things happened. Firstly, many inhabitants of the village arrived to see if they could help, secondly, pair of typical fire engine klaxon in the greenhouse was set off, and, lastly, another alarm is triggered in the local police station, causing the police to arrive in force, together with fire engines and ambulances, obviously at considerable public expense. It was therefore hardly surprising when after the second false alarm we received a stern warning letter from the police, saying that they operated a 'three strikes and you are out' policy. We have therefore adopted a policy of covering up the red buttons when there are children around, and keeping the emergency panic button at a location we know about but no one else does, except for our visiting housekeeper.

East Dean is one of three local villages served by the same vicar. Our most recent clergyman, Richard Wood (just retired), who in earlier life was an accountant (so he is well-qualified to serve both God and Mammon) shocked the rather low-church villagers by wearing on arrival what appeared to be a biretta, which smacked of Roman Catholicism. However, I got on with him rather well, though I never (because of my ancestry) attended any of his services, except to show some sort of solidarity with the local inhabitants, on Christmas Eve. So, one day I asked him why he had committed this social solecism. He replied

"That's not a biretta – it's a Thomas More cap!"

I didn't see that that made much difference, since Thomas More was an opponent of the Protestant cause, and was executed for treason by Henry VIII for refusing to accept that monarch as supreme head of the Church of England. Richard Wood's wife, Jane, was Head of Mathematics at Chichester High School for Girls. Richard and the villagers await anxiously the hoped-for appointment of his successor. However, there is apparently some doubt about this, since the Church of England is, like many organisations, currently somewhat strapped for cash.

A few miles from us is the small town of Arundel, the main street of which is a steep hill, lined with shops on one side and high walls on the other. The town is dominated by the huge Arundel Castle, seat of the Duke of Norfolk. At the bottom of the hill, by the River Arun, are the gardens of the Wildfowl and Wetlands Trust, which contains a remarkable collection of birds, both free-living and caged, and from many parts of the world as well as the UK. Once, at the entrance, there was a sudden flash of blue and a kingfisher plunged into the local waterway, emerging with a fish in its bill. The only other place where I have seen these beautiful creatures is in Wharfedale in Yorkshire, where, if are you are sufficiently still and in commune with Nature, a kingfisher may alight on the tip of your fishing rod.

Across the road from Spring Cottage was the rather bigger house in the middle of a large garden, which we had our eye on, but it was at that time lived in by an elderly widowed lady who had a Philippino nurse/housekeeper called Boon, and a dog. In due course the widow, whose husband had manufactured spare parts for fire-engines, was taken unto her fathers, leaving Boon and the dog in this enormous house. It seemed to us that the house we had our eye on, Longmeadow, would come on to the market at any moment, but this was not the apparently to be the case. It turned out that the lady's will had specified that the house was not to be sold until the dog died! (I had dark intentions of pulling out my AK 47 and shooting the dog at the dead of night, but never had the guts to do this!) Eventually the dog did die of natural causes, and we were able to buy the property at bargain price, since the housing market happened to be in the doldrums at that time. Readers should know that I am President, Secretary, Treasurer and sole member of the World Society of Dog Haters. There is much more to this antipathy than our protracted wait in Spring Cottage. Why do I harbour this particular prejudice? Well, the wretched creatures leap up, slobber all over you, lick your face, pee on your boots, crap on your lawn and trip you over with their leads! (cats forever!) Unfortunately, most of our friends in East Dean have dogs, and, in order to prevent myself carrying out my murderous intentions, I have to pretend that they are sheep. One of the few disadvantages of East Dean is its liability to flooding in wet weather. The village pond and green disappear, fountains of water spray out of all the drain covers in the streets and eventually raw sewage appears. The local children think all this is great fun and play with their toy sailing boats in the effluent!

Longmeadow was in a pretty poor state of repair when we moved in, as I have said, and we had to have some construction work done, including re-tiling the roof and some much needed interior decoration. Longmeadow is about four feet above the level of the street, but water runs down off the hill behind us and gets under the floor boards. We have a number of lengths of hose which we use to syphon this water out of a sump (which is connected with the underfloor space) down the 60 yard drive. The syphon is initiated by back filling the hoses; Barbara, being the daughter of a water engineer, is especially expert at this task (when we owned Spring Cottage, which was also vulnerable to flooding, as a weekend retreat, we used to put all the armchairs and other vulnerable furniture on the dining room table when leaving for Beckenham on a Sunday evening).

The general ethos of the area is illustrated by the fact that the signpost at Singleton indicates the distances to the various pubs up the valley, rather than those to the villages therein! We are well-endowed with pubs providing good food, and we divide our custom between 'The Partridge' at Singleton, 'The Fox Goes Free' at Charlton and 'The Star and Garter' at East Dean. The 'Star and Garter' is decorated with dried hops, shotgun cartridges and ancient sepia photographs, and has a well, useful for gauging the height of the water table during times of potential flooding. When serious flooding occurs, water squirts up in small fountains through their well, and much of our garden becomes like a small lake. A torrent also emerges from under the 'Star and Garter'. Under these circumstances the locals are apt to remark

"The Springs are up!"

When we first bought Spring Cottage, we thought that its name referred to a season of the year, a mistake revealed when waterspouts appeared in the front drive!

East Dean lies in a valley in the South Downs; also in this valley are the villages of Charlton and Singleton. The Fox Goes Free, referred to above, is famous for a meeting held in the early years of the last century, to initiate the formation of what has become the national Women's Insititutes. East Dean is connected with the main road from Chichester to Petworth by the very narrow Droke Lane (with passing places). When we first lived in East Dean progress was frequently impeded by flocks of red-legged partridges, which were wandering in search of nourishment. When they were approached by a car they tried to escape by running in front of the vehicle, and, not surprisingly, the lane was often littered with the corpses of squashed partridges. But, some twelve years later, the partridges of the day had the sense to fly off into the hedge and save themselves. We thought that this was an excellent example of Darwinian natural selection in action. Clearly, during the course of these twelve years, a mutation must have occurred which gave them the sense to fly off, and only those with the mutation had thus survived, thus giving rise to today's more sensible animal!

The most distinguished resident of East Dean when we arrived was the poet and dramatist Christopher Fry, author of "*The Dark is Light Enough*", "*The Boy with a Cart*", "*The Lady's Not for Burning*" and "*Venus Observed*". As with all new residents he invited us to tea so that he could get our measure! He used to give occasional talks in East Dean Village Hall, and when, at one of these, when he was aged over ninety, he was asked by a member of the audience

"Christopher, what is your prescription for a long life?"

He immediately replied

"Avoid all salads!"

He is buried with his wife Phyllida, in East Dean Church graveyard, at a site of his choosing, looking down the valley to Charlton and Singleton and to Chichester in the far distance. His work presumably caused Margaret Thatcher, who was trying to inspire some determination amongst those present at the Conservative Party Conference in 1980 to declare

"You turn if you want to, but the lady's not for turning!"

Bosham is a nearby village where we sailed in our youth and we revisited an old haunt, The Millstream Hotel, for Barbara's eightieth birthday party with the family recently (Plate 12). Luckily, though this happened on a cold winter's day, the tide was not up and we could walk and park where we liked. At high tide this is a notorious trap, because the sea floods up into the streets and submerges any car left near the sea by drivers foolish enough not have read the warning signs before parking.

Petworth has an enormous mansion (Petworth House), the seat of the Egremonts, which contains an excellent art collection, with many original works by JMW Turner, who spent some time in residence there, painting the local scenery. These include many views of Petworth Park and its herds of deer, as well as some more unusual interior scenes. Amongst them is his "*Chichester Canal*", a print of which hung in my rooms at Cambridge for many years, and which we still have in our guest annexe. In this painting, the sun has almost set over the South Down, and Turner has depicted this by a small depression in the sky line over the top of the Downs, a quite magical and ingenious effect.

Chichester Cathedral is a rather magnificent edifice; apart from its classical gothic architecture its spire is the home of peregrine falcons, which occasionally swoop down to grab some food; it is therefore advisable not to eat your sandwiches with your mouth open in the streets of the city! The courtyard of Chichester Cathedral is graced by a statue by Philip Jackson of Saint Richard (1197-1253), the patron saint of the city. The latter had a turbulent life; he studied for the priesthood at Oxford, and, because of his learning and piety was appointed Chancellor of the University. He fell out with King Henry III when he was appointed by St. Edmund of Canterbury in preference to a worthless candidate put forward by the King. The King refused to recognise his election to the bishopric and seized the revenues of the diocese, which were only restored two years later. Though St. Richard was generally loved, he was pretty stern in his punishment of transgressors. Thus when a knight forcefully imprisoned a priest, St. Richard compelled the erring knight to walk around the priest's compound with the same log of wood around his neck as that to which he had chained the priest during his incarceration. The churches in those days used to act as sanctuaries for all and sundry, including criminals. When the citizens of Lewes tore a certain criminal from a church and hanged him, Richard made them dig up his body from its unconsecrated grave and take it back to the church from which he had been snatched. He died whilst he was preaching to rally support for a Crusade in the Holy Land against the Saracens.

Philip Jackson, the sculptor of St. Richard, recently had an exhibition of his works in a local park (West Dean Gardens). The exhibition was dominated by his portrayal of Venetian grandees, who had golden faces and curious hands emerging out of sleeves with gold linings. He has also done some more conventional work, including a life sized statue of Bobby Moore, the captain of England's football team when they won the World Cup in 1966, and of Raoul Wallenberg (1912-1947), a Swedish diplomat who organised the rescue of tens of thousands of Jews from Nazi-occupied Hungary during the Holocaust. In this respect, Wallenberg resembled Oskar Schindler (1908-1974), a German business man who saved hundreds of Polish Jews from the Nazis during World War II by employing them in his enamelling factory. He had struck up friendships with high-ranking officers in the Wehrmacht and the SS by supplying them with cigars and cognac and this blinded them to what he was actually up to. He bribed the local commandant, Amon Goeth, to allow him to move his factory and workers to Czechoslovakia, so that he could continue to provide the

German army with 'vital supplies'. Goeth asked Schindler to draw up a list of whom he wanted to take with him; the list Schindler constructed contained about 1100 names. About 300 women and children were mistakenly routed to Auschwitz instead of to Brunnlitz, but Schindler managed to rescue these. In 1962 he went to Jerusalem and planted a tree in the avenue leading up to the Yad Vashem memorial to the victims of the Holocaust. The Australian author, Thomas Kenneally, wrote a Booker Prize winning novel (*"Schindler's Ark"*) in 1982; the book was later used by Steven Spielberg as the basis for his Oscar-winning film *"Schindler's List"*. When Schindler eventually died he was buried in the Catholic cemetery on Mount Zion in Israel. During a visit we made to Poland recently we visited the factory that he ran, which has a museum devoted to his work. Unlike Warsaw, which was almost totally destroyed by the Germans in World War II, Cracow was intact, since the German army had been billeted there during the war, and had no time to blow it up before being conquered.

Barbara is much addicted to the music of Benjamin Britten, since he and Peter Pears used to visit the boarding school at Melksham where she was a pupil. They were friends of her music teacher, Rudi Sabor, and they always gave a concert during these visits. The pupils learnt several of Britten's compositions, including the *"Ceremony of Carols"* and many of his folk songs. I was less bowled over, but did quite like his *"Sea Idylls"*. We once made a visit to the Snape Maltings Concert Hall in Aldeburgh, Suffolk. The construction of the hall was inspired by Britten himself. This part of the Suffolk coast is particularly cold and bleak, which, I suppose, fits in well with the tragic nature of his opera *"Peter Grimes"* and, to my mind, the general effect of his music. Rudi Sabor was a great admirer of the music of Richard Wagner and wrote many well-known monographs describing and commenting upon his operas.

 Our most recent visit was to Crete, where we hired a car for touring around the island. The first stop was the town of Chania, which was mildly (but not very) interesting, our only lasting memory being the considerable inconvenience of the apartment we had rented for a few days. It had no less than four floors, accessed by staircases which had no banisters. The ground floor was the lobby, the next the sitting room, followed by the bedroom and then the bathroom facilities. We then moved on to Kapsaliana, a village set in an olive grove; our hotel had its own museum, which boasted an 18th century olive press, and equipment for extracting the oil from the olives and storing it. The final port of call was Aghios Nikolaos, a seaside resort, whose main interest was its proximity to Spinalonga (Plate 13), an island a mile or two off the coast. Spinalonga acted as a leper colony established by order of the Greek Government from 1903 to 1957, when it became redundant because of the use of the drug dapsone, an effective cure for the disease for many years, until resistance to the drug developed. It is the subject of a novel by Victoria Hislop ("*The Island*"), which describes the distress of lepers and their families at their forcible parting. Leprosy is a very ancient disease, the condition being recognised in ancient China, Egypt and India. It was recognised as a disease in England, possibly as early as the fifth century ad. Those afflicted were required to ring a bell whilst walking the streets, calling out "Unclean, unclean" at intervals to warn passers-by to keep their distance. Leprosy featured in the blockbuster film '*Ben Hur*', when the hero, after returning from the wars, found that his family had vanished; eventually he located them in a leper colony. Modern therapy overcomes the difficulty of the development of resistance by the use of triple therapy, (consisting of rifampicin, dapsone and clofazine) taken over a period of a year. In this it very much resembles the problem of treating tuberculosis, which perhaps is not surprising since the causative agent, *Mycobacterium leprae*, comes from the same group of bacteria as does that causing tuberculosis. Leprosy is also known as 'Hansen's Disease', after the discoverer of the bacterium, Gerhard Hansen (1841-1912), who was born in Bergen, the centre for Norwegian leprosy research. He was an assistant physician at the Lungagegaardshospitalet, working under a Dr. Daniel Danielsen. The latter believed that leprosy was hereditary, an idea held by many physicians of the day, which was, of course disproved by Hansen's discovery of *M. leprae*. One might imagine that Hansen would have been treated with respect after this discovery, but he was in fact pilloried by the Norwegian clergy for his support for Charles Darwin's 'blasphemous views' on evolution.

Barbara and I once spent a holiday in Norway, sailing up the coast on a steamer belonging to the Hurtigrüten service, whose main function was to deliver the mail and freight to those parts of the country most easily accessed by sea. One entertainment provided by the captain was to sail up an extremely narrow fjord, whose width was only a few feet greater the length of the boat. The passengers, including ourselves, thought that he would have to reverse out; in fact, he executed a perfect multi-point turn and sailed out bow-first, to tremendous applause from the passengers. The boat also called at Svolvaer, a fishing town at the foot of the Lofoten archipelago. We drove out along the archipelago over a series of inter-connecting bridges, to the town at the end – Å – which must surely be the shortest name of any town on the globe; I believe it is pronounced "aw". I did a watercolour and gouache painting of Henningsvaer in the Lofoten Islands (Plate 14); the white buildings with red roofs on the right are charnel houses stuffed to the ceiling with dried salted cod, this being a winter food reserve when the seas were too rough for successful fishing. We also visited Narvik, over which many engagements were fought during World War II. This town is a port high up on the coast of Norway and was used by the Germans to collect iron ore mined in the Kiruna (see below) district, the iron being essential for the German armament factories. The port provided a deep anchorage which was virtually ice free during winter. During 1940 the Germans sent a number of destroyers to Narvik, each carrying 200 soldiers. The Norwegian coastal defence ships were quickly sunk by these destroyers, which were, in turn, destroyed by a British force led by the battleship *HMS Warspite*. However, the German battleships *Scharnhorst* and *Gneisenau* managed to sink the British aircraft carrier, *HMS Glorious*. British troops were landed near Narvik and recaptured the city in May, 1940. Narvik also was a haven for the German battleship *Tirpitz*, which was menacing convoys of arms to the Soviet Union, and the Royal Navy had to maintain substantial forces in the area to contain this threat. The *Tirpitz* was eventually destroyed in a raid by Lancaster bombers, which dropped 12,000 pound 'Tallboy' bombs, after unsuccessful raids by mini-submarines; these vessels had slipped under the anti-torpedo nets in the fjord, and they succeeded in attaching time-fused mines whose detonation damaged the *Tirpitz*, but not beyond repair. Finally, a well-known Norwegian artist, Espolin Johnson (1907-1994), has done a number of extremely gloomy paintings of fisherman; one of these show the men hauling up their nets, whilst in the background are ghostly images of their comrades who have drowned (Plate 15). These were displayed in a gallery of his works. The general sombreness was, however, relieved by a small boy who was sitting at a piano playing Mozart's "*Rondo alla Turca*" with enormous gusto (the third movement of his Piano Sonata No.1).

I have referred above to the wartime history of Kiruna, which is in the Lapland region of North Scandinavia. A rather lighter hearted event occurred there more recently involving our son, Martin, who had gone to Kiruna as part of some event set up by the International Space University. We received a telephone call from him in which he complained loudly that

"I'm staying in an ice hotel, which is fascinating, but I'm driving around on a sled drawn by reindeer, sleeping in a tent made of reindeer pelts, on a ground sheet made of reindeer skin, keeping warm by a fire made of reindeer dung, eating reindeer meat, and reindeer are trying to break into my room!"

We visited Poland roughly two years ago and before leaving had applied to the UK Foreign Office for tips on visiting Poland. The information they sent us warned us to be especially vigilant with regard to thieves who haunted railway stations. So, when we boarded a train at Cracow bound for Warsaw, Barbara kept everything valuable in a 'bumbag' hidden under her jacket. However, as we boarded with our three bags, they were grabbed by some men who were also boarding. Whilst struggling to keep hold of the bags, Barbara managed to keep hold of the one containing especially valuable items by holding it above her head whilst climbing the steps into the carriage. This allowed one of the gang to neatly remove her bumbag and run off, unnoticed. Some ten minutes after the train had left Cracow, she suddenly became aware that her bumbag was missing. Apart from money, it also contained her passport. We realised with horror that Barbara was now effectively a 'stateless person'. Fortunately, about ten minutes after the train's departure, a stewardess appeared wielding the missing bumbag, which she had found dumped in a carriage several coaches down and enquiring if anyone was the owner. So we gratefully got Barbara's passport back as the thieves had not taken it, but some three hundred pounds worth of Polish zlotys had, of course, vanished, together with credit and debit cards. Fortunately, by that time we had already called up the debit and credit card companies and cancelled these cards. We reported this incident to the police in Warsaw and spent the whole morning at the local police station waiting for someone to appear who could speak English, but they seemed rather bored by the whole incident. We were eventually rescued by a bellboy from our hotel who had learnt English at school.

One of the most memorable but harrowing excursions on this visit was to Auschwitz-Birkenau, where more than one million Jews, gypsies and other 'undesirables' were murdered. We had engaged a lady about forty years old to conduct us around what is now effectively a museum of The Holocaust. She took us through the entrance arch with the inscription "*Arbeit Macht Frei!*" in large iron letters overhead and down to the gas chambers through the roofs of which canisters of the cyanide-generating substance Cyklon B had been dropped by the guards. There were several rooms devoted to the exhibition of the hair and teeth of the victims, and their shoes, clothes, spectacles and bones. She then took us to the incinerators which had been used for disposal of the corpses. We asked our guide how long she had been doing this job. She replied

"About fifteen years."

When asked how she could have stood it for so long, she replied

"I regard it as my duty."

She then took us to the office of the commandant, Rudolf Höss, who joined the Nazi party in 1922 and the SS in 1934. He was hanged in 1947 following his trial in Warsaw. We also learnt that Auschwitz itself was a makeshift set-up, but that the adjacent Birkenau had been purpose-built by the Nazis. The barracks existing at that time to house the Nazi guards had been turned into a memorial of organised devastation at the end of the railway line that brought victims for execution.

I have made several attempts in the past, all rejected, to have a paper published in *The Quarterly Journal of Medicine (QJM)*, published by Oxford University Press. All the rejected papers had eventually got into journals with a similar or higher 'impact factor', so I was forced to conclude that their attitude was part of the Dark Blue/Light Blue rivalry, and that my Cambridge associations had turned them off! However, to my amazement I then got a short paper accepted by the *QJM*. This was a somewhat tongue-in-cheek effort, provoked by the fact that that the soles of my feet are very sensitive. I had noticed that walking on sand is entirely comfortable, but as I got on to the larger pebbles, it very rapidly became rather painful. When ground elements approached paving stone size, matters slowly improved. In other words, a graph of the level of discomfort experienced against the size of components underfoot was biphasic, with an initial steep rise to a peak, followed by a slow decline to virtually zero. It was possible to fit the curve by the following equation:

$$D = 1.9(k/\lambda).(x/\lambda)^{k-1}.e^{-(x/\lambda)k}$$

where D is a measure of distress scaled from 0 (perfectly comfortable) to 1 (agonising), and k and λ in this case are 1.5 and 1, respectively. This is an example of the Weibull distribution described by Waloddi Weibull (1887-1979), who was born in Schleswig-Holstein, at that time closely connected with Denmark. He worked in Swedish and German universities and invented ball and roller bearings and an electric hammer. He spent time as a member of the crew of the research ship '*Albatross*' and used explosive charges to determine the nature of the ocean floor, in a way somewhat reminiscent of the sonar techniques used in anti-submarine warfare.

I was once at a concert in Chichester Cathedral and found myself sitting next to the Lord Mayor of that city. During the interval I complained to him about the state of the city's pavements and cobblestone alleys, and suggested to him that he might bring up the subject at the next meeting of the Town Council. Instead of taking this request on board, he started pointing out to me the great success he had achieved in getting rid of the graffiti on the city walls. This is an excellent example of the technique, much beloved by politicians, of the alternative proposition, ably expounded in JM Cornford's "*Microcosmographica Academia*". This proposition states that a good way in committee of preventing something happening is to get some of your colleagues to make alternative proposals. This creates such confusion that the likely outcome is that nothing happens at all! Devotees of the TV serial "*Yes, Minister*" will recognise the technique often employed by the Permanent Secretary, Sir Humphrey Appleby. Finally, on this topic, I once had a patient with the syndrome of total lipodystrophy. In this condition, there is complete absence of subcutaneous fat. The consequence is that all the outlines of the muscles of the arms and legs are clearly visible through the skin and the cheeks are hollow, like someone suffering from starvation. Since there is no fat padding to the soles of the feet, walking around towns in the present state of our towns and cities must be incredibly painful for a person with this condition.

After my retirement I managed to complete one paper which I regard as one of my better efforts. The story of this paper arises from the time when I was Senior Censor and Vice President of the Royal College of Physicians. I have already referred to the Presidential Business Discussions held monthly, at which the finest of wines were served, as already mentioned, but I did not say that when drinking them I used to experience a warm feeling under the right costal margin. Some might say that this was purely psychological – induced by the fact that someone other than myself was paying for the wine (i.e. the Fellows and Members of the College through their annual subscriptions). But in fact there turned out to be a probable physiological, rather than psychological, reason for this phenomenon, and it came to me what it might be whilst I was soaking in a hot bath one night. It is necessary to remind readers here of the microstructure of the liver. Plate 6 shows the normal liver lobule; there are radial strings of hepatocytes extending between the surface of the lobule and the hepatic venule in the centre. These strings are separated by the hepatic sinusoids which carry the blood from the radicals of the portal vein and hepatic artery in the portal tracts to the hepatic venule in the centre of each lobule. The set-up may be drawn diagrammatically as a series of closely packed adjacent circles. This inevitably leaves triangular spaces between the circles, and these triangles have concave sides. Such spaces may be seen on the roofs of many cathedrals, separating adjacent domes and are known as 'spandrels'. Plate 16 shows the ceiling of one such cathedral.

Going somewhat more deeply into this, if one considers the radial structure of the liver lobule, the blood flows centripetally in the sinusoids, from the portal tracts on the outside, to the hepatic venule in the centre, it is obvious that the linear rate of blood flow must greatly increase towards the centre of the lobule. This means that the cells near the hepatic venule have much less time to perform their functions than do the peripheral periportal cells, because the blood rapidly vanishes into the hepatic venule, and thence into the hepatic vein and the inferior vena cava. This is the sort of inefficiency which Nature tends to sort out during the long process of evolution. A possible mechanism to compensate for this would be for the temperature to rise progressively in a centripetal direction along the radius of the liver lobule. The high temperature in the more central cells would speed up the rate of biochemical reactions within them, so we set out to measure the temperature change along the radius. The most obvious approach would be to insert micro-thermocouples, and we obtained (at considerable expense) a set of these from Nanonics, an Israeli company. However, they proved to be very fragile and kept on breaking; furthermore, we realised they were damaging the very tissues whose temperatures we were trying to measure. There is a clear analogy with Heisenberg's famous Uncertainty Principle, which states that there is a fundamental limitation to the precision with which, in regard to a subatomic particle, its position and momentum can be measured at the same time. So we had to have recourse to more indirect methods. We firstly created a mathematical model of heat transfer down the radius of the lobule; some of the mathematics involved was a bit beyond me, so I approached Adrian Smith, who was at that time Principal of Queen Mary College, just down the Mile End Road from

The London Hospital, for advice. He thought it over and then declared that the man whose talents we needed was Wen Wang, Professor of Biomedical Engineering at Queen Mary. We started by assuming intuitively that any heat generated in exothermic reactions in the periphery of the lobule was carried down the sinusoid almost entirely in the sinusoidal blood, and not by diffusion through the liver cells themselves. This leads to the following equation of heat transfer:-

$$T = T_a + (Vq)/Fs.[1 - (r/a)^3]$$

where V is the volume of a lobule, F the blood flow rate at the entry to the sinusoid, q is the rate of heat production per unit volume of tissue, s is the specific heat of the tissue and r is the radial distance of the cell under consideration from the centre of the lobule (where r = 0), and a is the value of r at the surface of the lobule. It turned out that even when the temperature coefficient of reaction rate for each 10°C rise (Q_{10}) is as high as five, temperature rise along the sinusoid was only about 1.12°C, which was unlikely to make much difference to the rate of membrane transport and subsequent metabolism. So it became clear that that some other mechanism had to be involved. A possible mechanism would be if there was a high concentration of an uncoupling protein (UCP) in the centrilobular cells (there are several varieties of UCP, the one relevant to the liver being UCP2). Uncoupling proteins have the property of preventing the storage of energy derived from the electron transfer chain as ATP; instead, it is released as heat, and this was just what we were looking for. So, in cooperation with my late colleague Christopher Brown, who was an expert at immuno-histochemistry, we examined histological sections of liver to establish the location of UCP2. We found it to be highly concentrated in the centrilobular cells (Plate17). In order to provide evidence that the reason for the centrilobular location of UCP2 was indeed to do with the need to raise temperature, we also examined the location of another protein, transient receptor potential version 4 (TRPv4) (Plate 18), a membrane channel constituent known to have an unusually high Q_{10}. We found UCP2 and TRPv4 to be precisely co-located, and this was strong evidence that the reason for the centrilobular concentration of UCP2 was indeed to raise the temperature of centrilobular cells. The detailed mathematics involved in the derivation of the equation of heat transfer given above may be found in the original paper[5].

There are some interesting possible consequences of centrilobular warming, arising from the fact that UCP2 has a number of genetic polymorphisms, some of which increase its function, whilst others have the opposite effect. A loss-of-function polymorphism, which cooled the centrilobular cells, would, for instance, decrease the activity of the enzyme glucokinase, which normally takes up glucose from the sinusoidal blood and either stores it as glycogen, or uses it to fuel other metabolic reactions. It might therefore contribute to the pathogenesis of Type 2 diabetes by allowing more glucose to reach the circulation than is normally the case. A gain-of-function UCP2 polymorphism might eventually harm the centrilobular cells by repeated heating due to the metabolism of alcohol by alcohol dehydrogenase, which is most active in the centrilobular cells, and be responsible for the ultimate development of cirrhosis. This could account for the fact that only a minority of heavy drinkers develop cirrhosis, i.e. those who had the gain-of-function polymorphism. Work on these suggestions is in progress. For example, genome-wide association studies are showing that serum alanine amino-transferase, an indicator of liver cell damage, varies with the particular UCP2 polymorphism present in an alcohol drinker. What is missing so far is the demonstration that cirrhotics have a gain-of-function polymorphism. This possibility is currently being examined by Professor Elina Hypponen, of the Institute of Child Health, Great Ormond Street, London. Although there do not seem to be specific UCP2 polymorphisms linked to Type 2 diabetes, there is evidence that a gain-of-function glucokinase polymorphism is protective in respect of Type 2 diabetes. Again, what is so far missing is a demonstration that a loss-of-function glucokinase polymorphism is associated with an increased incidence of the common variety of Type 2 diabetes. These possibilities are currently under examination by Graham Hitman's group at The London.

On another Medical Pilgrims visit to the Czech Republic, we took the opportunity of paying homage to the memory of Gregor Mendel (1822-1884) in his garden at Brno. This was where he established his laws of inheritance by experiments on the hybridisation of different varieties of pea plants. Mendel was originally trained as a priest and such training, in those days of enlightenment, included the study of physics! He eventually rose to become abbot of the Augustinian Abbey of St. Thomas in Brno in 1884. He also bred bees in a personally designed hive, and studied astronomy and meteorology; the majority of his published works are, in fact, related to meteorology. I wonder if he made a better job of it than is sometimes the case for our own Meteorological Office?

Amongst our chief occupations since we retired has been visiting countries to which we had never previously been. One of these was Israel, where we bobbed around in the Dead Sea before taking the fresh water showers provided on the shores to enable one to wash off the salt. Having thus cleansed ourselves we moved off to Jerusalem. Wandering around the city gave me a somewhat eerie feeling, as there were all sorts of curious characters to be seen including many ultra-orthodox Jews, whose '*pais*' (side-locks) were so long that they had to be bound by a belt round the waist to keep them from getting tangled up with animate or inanimate objects in the vicinity of their owner. Most of these people were making for the Wailing Wall, Judaism's holiest site, where they prayed with the characteristic swaying backwards and forwards (known in Yiddish as '*shokelling*') seen in synagogues during the routine recital of prayers. After finishing their devotions, they thrust pieces of paper into cracks in the Wall; I am not sure what was written on these bits of paper. We then moved on to the Dome of the Rock (the third most holy place in Israel after Mecca and Medina) and took our shoes off before entering, adding them to the enormous pile of other visitors' shoes. We then toiled up the steps past the Twelve Stations of the Cross to The Church of the Holy Sepulchre near Golgotha, the site of the Crucifixion, which is shared between the Catholic, Greek Orthodox and Armenian branches of Christianity before we moved on to Bethlehem, where there were enormous queues of people waiting to see the alleged place of Christ's birth. When we finally got in, we found tableaux of the manger and Mary suckling the infant Jesus. We moved on to the site on the River Jordan where Christ was baptised. There were pilgrims dressed in white gowns immersing themselves in the river, which turned out to be a rather insignificant stream containing golden carp. This part of the visit involved crossing into the Palestinian-controlled area, where armed border guards were carefully scrutinising the crowds for any undesirable behaviour. We had a look at the Dead Sea Scrolls, discovered by some shepherds in a cave at Qumran. Some of the scrolls (there were 972 of them altogether, including those found in other caves in the area) are in the Israel Museum in Jerusalem; these are written on parchment in ancient Hebrew, and I found these fairly easy to read, much more so than the modern Hebrew ('*Ivrit*') used in Israel today. Others are in Aramaic, Greek and Nabatean, and have been dated using radioactive carbon and other analyses to between 318 and 408bc. Incidentally, in most Jewish circles, the abbreviations ace and bce are used rather than ad and bc. The latter, of course stand for '*anno domini*' and 'before Christ', but some of the more prejudiced Jews refuse to use these Christian terms, believing that most of the sufferings endured in the Diaspora have been due to massacres perpetrated by alleged Christians. bce and ace stand for before and after the Common Era, respectively. Finally, we visited Masada, a piece of ground 300 ft high and only accessible via narrow winding paths. Masada was the site of a battle between Jewish rebels and their Roman masters in 73ad. 960 Jews were confronted by 15,000 Roman troops, equipped with a siege tower and a battering ram. When the Romans finally prevailed, they found that the Jews had committed mass suicide.

About three years ago we did a tour of some of the Balkan countries, including Slovenia, Croatia, Serbia, Montenegro and Albania. Everyone knows of the turbulent history of this region throughout the centuries, but during our visit it was a haven of peace! It had recovered from the rule of its notorious communist ruler, Enver Hoxha (1908-1985), who was a Communist despot in the Stalin mode. He ruled for forty years, systematically eliminating any opposition by death or imprisonment. Since he was anti-fascist, he received support during World War II from British Special Operations Executive (SOE). One of the places we went to was Kotor, in Montenegro. This town is built on the side of a very steep hill, which presents a variety of construction problems. Plate 19 shows the technique that the inhabitants adopt for roof repairs. Two workers are involved, the first being the anchor-man, who holds the rope tied around the waist of the second, who is actually doing the work. I don't suppose they have too much in the way of the UK Health and Safety at work legislation! Note also the washing hanging on the line; it certainly adds colour to the generally drab scenery. We also went to Tirana (Albania) where there is a magnificent National Museum, both architecturally and in terms of a good deal of its content.

Barbara had a close friend at her school, named Stella, who later married Gerald Butler, a judge. Gerald died recently, but Stella still maintains their weekend cottage in Fowey, a small town in the southern end of Cornwall. Gerald was extremely fond of oysters; he used to take me to the village fish merchant, and invited me to join him in swallowing these molluscs in one gulp, which I just about managed to do without retching. Fowey is also a base for the local lifeboat, which is moored in front of Stella's cottage. It seemed quite frequently to be called out, but presumably on most of these occasions this was a training and maintenance exercise. There are two means of getting to Fowey by car. One is a rather circuitous road route, but much quicker is the ferry from Bodinnick across the Fowey River. When we first started visiting Fowey, the ferry consisted of a few planks bound together, attached to the side of a motor boat, on to which you drove your car. It would only take up to three cars, depending on their size, and the queues to get on were often enormous. Furthermore, as you drove on, the whole contraption tended to tip over and deposit the cars and their passengers into the river! This death trap has now been replaced by a proper ferry which takes a large number of vehicles, and the queues have largely vanished. Opposite the mouth of the Fowey River is the village of Polruan, which is built on one of the steepest hills in the country. It is provided with sandpits to run into if your brakes should fail.

Most readers will be aware that the pavements of most towns are heavily polluted with blobs of discarded chewing gum, which, if recently deposited, tend to stick to the soles of one's shoes, and the process of removing it is quite disgusting! I once made a simple calculation which demonstrated that the four main thoroughfares of Chichester – North, East, West and South Streets – had at least 40,000 blobs of chewing gum deposited on them. I have often wondered whether any of the common contagious disease are acquired from these blobs. Gerald Butler was quite convinced that the blobs were seagull droppings; eventually I persuaded him of the truth by threatening to scrape off one of these blobs and have it analysed for uric acid, which is the end-product of metabolism of purine compounds (e.g. DNA) in birds, in contrast to urea in most mammals. Higher primates, including humans, excrete uric acid in the urine as such, rather than oxidise it to the highly soluble allantoin, as is done in most mammals. If large amounts of uric acid or its salts are excreted by the kidney they may crystallise out to form stones in some part of the urinary tract. Dalmatian dogs are prone to uric acid stone formation because they have a liver cell membrane transport defect resulting in insufficient supply of the enzyme uricase, which converts uric acid into the very soluble allantoin. They are distinguished from other types of stone (e.g. calcium or cystine-containing) by being completely transparent to X-rays, and, therefore, only become visible on X-rays if the radiographs are taking after the injection of some contrast medium. If that is done, the stone is outlined by a thin layer of the contrast, and it becomes obvious that stones are present. Fortunately, urate stones are amongst the easiest to treat, since they are very soluble at alkaline pH values. So the administration of sufficient sodium bicarbonate to raise the urinary pH to its maximum possible value of 7.7-8.0 is often all that is needed. Lastly on the subject of chewing gum, someone had stuck a lump of the stuff inside the bannister of the four flights of stairs up to the ward where I worked at The London. Since the lifts were always full, I used to climb the stairs and for forty years or more my hand came into daily contact with this lump of gum. However, just before my retirement it dropped off, an event which I attributed to a bereavement reaction on the part of the lump of gum!

My health had been pretty good during my early and working life, apart from the episodes of pulmonary tuberculosis and gout that I have already mentioned. But things began to get more difficult in the early days of my retirement. One day I was leaning against a table, when I felt a buzzing sensation in my chest (known technically as a 'thrill'). I got Barbara to listen with her stethoscope and to her horror she heard a loud murmur early in diastole, a classical sign of aortic valve regurgitation. This means that much of the blood ejected into the ascending aorta by the left ventricle flows back into the ventricle during diastole. Initially, I had no idea why I should have this problem, since I didn't have syphilis, nor had I ever suffered from rheumatic fever, these being the usual causes, but eventually the penny dropped. It was probably due to taking ergotamine for my frequent attacks of migraine; ergotamine is well-known to cause trouble with the pulmonary valve, but it less commonly affects the aortic valve. When I stopped the ergotamine, the migraines vanished! Ergotism has caused much more serious problems in the past. It is produced by a fungus (*Claviceps purpurea*) which infects rye and other cereals. Ingestion of ergot alkaloids produces painful seizures and spasms, diarrhoea, psychosis, paraesthesia and, believe it or not, headaches! It also produces dry gangrene of the extremities, due to vasoconstriction. It is also known as 'St. Anthony's Fire' because monks of the order of St. Anthony were apparently particularly successful at treating this disorder. In the notorious Salem Witch Trials, which took place in Massachusetts in 1692-93, there was much argument as to whether the symptoms exhibited by women accused of witchcraft were due to the work of the Devil, or were the result of some more prosaic affliction such as ergotism. St. Anthony (*circa* 251-356AD) himself is appealed to particularly by believers who are afflicted with ergotism, shingles and erysipelas.

When my aortic regurgitation was discovered, I went to see a cardiac surgeon named Steve Edmondson, who worked at the Wellington Hospital in Hampstead. He said that I should have the valve replaced very soon, before I went into serious heart failure. He then discussed the options for this replacement – either using a pig valve or a metallic ball-in-cage valve. With regard to the pig valve, this would only require me to be anticoagulated for three months after the operation, but the average life of these valves was only five to seven years, and the whole thing would have to be done again. On the other hand, the metallic valve would last indefinitely but required permanent anti-coagulation, and there would be a permanent clicking noise in my chest with each heartbeat. Anti-coagulation has its own serious complications if not tightly controlled. Eventually I decided on the pig valve, and I duly had the operation that week (presumably rendering me permanently non-Kosher!), in order to strike before heart failure ensued. Later on, in 2004, I had an episode of back pain and vomiting which proved to be due to a coronary thrombosis for which a stent was inserted, but too late to prevent a myocardial infarct. This left me somewhat unwell and I came under the care of Dr Cliff Bucknall, a cardiologist practising at St. Thomas' and The London Bridge Hospital, who re-stented the lesion and took over my cardiac care. Later, I lost some more exercise tolerance. Dr Bucknall got his colleague Professor John Chambers, a well-known expert in visualization of the heart by echocardiography, to further practice his art on me. He showed that my *left ventricular ejection fraction had fallen since the initial damage from the heart attack, after which I had had a combined pacemaker defibrillator inserted under my left *pectoralis* muscle to avoid problems from the bouts of abnormal heart rhythm that can occur after heart attacks. The findings showed that I was suitable for having a resynchronising pacemaker/defibrillator device with a lead to each ventricle inserted so as to ensure that the right and left ventricles both contracted together rather than separately. This made an enormous improvement to my exercise tolerance, which has lasted ever since. The pacemaker gives me a regular pulse as detected at the wrist, but electrocardiograhy shows that the underlying rhythm is now atrial fibrillation where atrial contraction is disorganised. In this situation, clots can form and may pass to the brain, lungs and limbs with potentially disastrous consequences. So, I have had to be anti-coagulated for years (with the coumarin derivative warfarin) after all. Fortunately, it has proved fairly easy to control the level of my anti-coagulation. Barbara bought a piece of apparatus known as a *Coaguchec-XS* and can check my level of anti-coagulation at home as often as is necessary, with occasional measurements in the clinical laboratory at St. Richard's Hospital in Chichester by an entirely different method. The two types of measurement have always agreed very closely. The defibrillator has gone off several times since its insertion, sometimes in my sleep, unnoticed, once in Lucerne, once in Taiwan on top of what was then the highest building in the world, and once after walking the mile or so down the road to the pub, 'The Fox Goes Free', in the village of Charlton. When this happens, you feel as if you have been kicked in the chest by a horse! Analysis of these episodes has shown a number of common features, namely they always happen before food, when

I am dry, e.g. as a result of the diuretic furosemide (which I take to prevent recurrence of heart failure), if I go to sleep without using the CPAP (see below), especially if I am also hot and vasodilated. I therefore try to avoid getting into these situations.

Since the myocardial infarct I have also suffered from sleep apnoea, a condition in which, during sleep, the depth of breathing gradually increases to a maximum, then declines and stops altogether. During these periods, one may become seriously short of oxygen (i.e. hypoxia), which isn't very good for you, especially if you have heart problems. The treatment is to use a piece of equipment known as a CPAP (Continuous Positive Alveolar Pressure) machine, which you are attached to through a mask and hose pipe. If it senses you are not breathing properly, it compensates for this by blowing air at pressure into the hose. Since disturbances of heart rhythm are encouraged by hypoxia, it is important to avoid such episodes. Like most men, I tend to drop off after meals. If my head nods, I am promptly kicked by Barbara, who insists that I wear my CPAP apparatus to sleep. She also has found a device which I can wear behind one of my ears when in danger of falling asleep; if my head droops, it emits a penetrating screech, which instantly wakes me up. On my travels around the world I have to carry the CPAP with me; it used to be quite a heavy piece of equipment which practically dislocated my shoulder carrying it around, but it has been improved by the manufacturers so that it is now much smaller and more manageable.

Our daughter Susan qualified in medicine but after some years, having reached Registrar level, she gave it up to care for her family and to deal with major surgery for her scoliosis as well. She is an excellent musician and still plays the piano; being an unusually good sight reader she is able to do various tasks like accompanying pupils taking music exams. Her husband David Legg is a computer software engineer with twenty five years' experience, who has also given up the work he trained for, who has been ordained as a minister. It seems very likely that he will take over a parish based on the village of Lee Mill, very near my original home town, Plymouth.

Our son, Martin, is an electronic engineer working continuously for the company that has evolved from Marconi Research into Astrium, where he is engaged in developing radar systems of ever-decreasing size and weight for use on smaller and smaller satellites and aeroplanes. His wife, Teresa, worked for twenty five years as a nurse, specializing in paediatrics and burns, and becoming a sister in a major

Accident and Emergency Department locally, However, she too has moved on, retraining as a primary school teacher and she already has an established full-time post which, though very hard work, she is enjoying – especially since the recent Ofsted inspection gave her, and her school, complimentary reports.

We have five grandsons, but no granddaughters. Susan and David have three sons: Stephen (age twenty two) is doing a fourth year for a Masters degree in Physics at Oxford. What he intends to do with this training is not yet clear. He has already written a textbook of physics for 'A' level students. Philip (aged twenty) is reading Chemistry with Physics at Bristol, and the youngest of Susan's sons, Harry is only fifteen, but writes very well, and declares his intention of becoming a professional author. They have all inherited their grandmother's talent for music. Martin and Teresa have two sons, Samuel and Thomas, aged fifteen and thirteen respectively. Sam wants to be an architect, of the type that builds large scale projects such as bridges. Tom is an excellent artist with an interest in things biological, and produces very good drawings of all kinds. None of them show the slightest interest in pursuing a medical career; Barbara and I must have put them off for good! Fortunately, none of them look much like becoming international sportsmen or film stars. They are all (superficially) polite to their aged grandparents. We look forward to seeing how they all make out!

Reference

1) Cohen RD, Brown CL, Wang W, Nickols C, Levey P, Boucher BJ and Greenwald SE. Inbuilt mechanisms for overcoming functional problems inherent in hepatic microlobular structure. *Computational and Mathematical Methods in Medicine* 2011, 1-9, 2011

CURRICULUM VITAE

NAME:	Professor Robert Donald Cohen
	Married to Professor Barbara J. Boucher, one son and one daughter
ADDRESS:	Longmeadow, East Dean, Chichester, West Sussex, PO18 0JB.
DATE OF BIRTH:	11th October, 1933.
QUALIFICATIONS:	MA(Cantab), MD(Cantab), FRCP, FMedSci
EDUCATION:	

1947-51	Clifton College, Bristol
1951-54	Trinity College, Cambridge – Open Scholar
	1st Class Honours Part I, Natural Science Tripos
	1st Class Honours Part II, Natural Science Tripos (Physiology)
	Senior Scholar, Trinity College, Cambridge
1954-58	The London Hospital Medical College (LHMC) (Price Entrance Scholar)
1958	M.B., B.Chir. (Cantab)
1966	M.D. (Cantab)

CAREER

1958-59	House Physician, The Medical Unit, and House Surgeon, The Surgical Unit, The London Hospital
1959-60	House Physician, Royal Postgraduate Medical School (RPMS)
1960-65	Lecturer in Medicine, The London Hospital Medical (LHMC)
1960	Member of The Royal College of Physicians (Lond)
1967-69	Senior Lecturer in Medicine, LHMC
1967	Honorary Consultant Physician, The London Hospital
1969-74	Reader in Medicine, LHMC, University of London
1974-82	Professor of Metabolic Medicine, LHMC, University of London
1982-99	Professor of Medicine and Director of the Academic Medical Unit, LHMC, later (from 1995) St Bartholomew's and The London School of Medicine and Dentistry,Queen Mary and Westfield College, University of London
1997	CBE
1998	Fellow of the Academy of Medical Sciences
1999	Emeritus Professor of Medicine, University of London

BOARDS AND COMMITTEES

1973-75	Chairman of the Editorial Board of Clinical Science
1974-76	Chairman of the Secretary of State's Advisory Committee on Medical Computing
1976-80	Chairman of the Department of Health's Computer Research and Development Committee
1980	Member of Medical Advisory Panel, Infantile Hypercalcaemia/Williams Syndrome Foundation
1982-84	Chairman of Board of Studies in Nutrition, University of London
1983-90	Chairman of the Special Advisory Committee on General (Internal) Medicine, Joint Committee on Higher Medical Training
1985-88	Member, Medical Research Council (MRC) Systems Board Committee B
1984-86	Pro-Censor and Censor, Royal College of Physicians of London (RCP)
1986-88	Chairman, Department of Health (DHSS)/MRC Co-ordinating Committee on Magnetic Resonance Imaging
1987	Member of Academic Medicine Group, RCP
1988-89	Chairman, MRC/DHSS Monitoring Committee on Magnetic Resonance Imaging
1989-99	Vice-Chairman, Research Grants Committee, London Hospital Special Trustees
1988-95	University of London Representative on General Medical Council
1988-89	Member of Education Committee of General Medical Council
1988-93	Member of General Medical Council Working Party on Recommendations on Basic Medical Education (1988-93)
1988-91	Chairman, North East Thames Regional Research Committee
1989	Chairman, British Diabetic Association Research Support Review Body
1989-91	Member of Council, Imperial Cancer Research Fund
1990-92	Member of Systems Board, MRC, and Member of Health Services

	Research Committee
1991-94	Vice Chairman of Council, Imperial Cancer Research Fund
1991-93	1st Vice-President and Senior Censor, RCP (London).
1991-93	Chairman of Censors' Board, Royal College of Physicians of London
1992-98	Member of Committee, National Kidney Research Fund
1992-94	Chairman, Royal College of Physicians Working Party on Provision of Neurological Services in District General Hospitals
1992-94	Deputy Chairman, MRC Physiological Medicine and Infections Board
1992-94	Member, MRC Health Services and Public Health Research Board
1993-2000	Chairman, MRC Virucides Steering Committee
1994-95	Member, President's Advisory Committee, General Medical Council
1994	Member, Lister Institute.
1994-2001	Chairman of Council, Imperial Cancer Research Fund
1996-99	Chairman, MRC Trial Steering Committee for the United Kingdom Prospective Diabetes Study (UKPDS).
1996-99	Member of External Advisory Committee, US National Institutes of Health trial of therapy of lactic acidosis in malaria.
1997-2000	Member of Council, King Edward VII Hospital, Midhurst
1998-99	Chairman, MRC Intensive Therapy Working Party
1997-2000	Member, MRC Innovation Grants Panel
1997-2005	Member of Academic and Research Committee, Specialist Training Authority
2000	Member of Infrastructure Grants Panel, Canada Foundation for Innovation
2000-02	Treasurer, Medical Research Society
2001-04	Member, School Development Group, Bart's and The London Bart's and The London School of Medicine and Dentistry
2001-02	Joint Chairman, Imperial Cancer Research Fund Research Campaign Merger Steering Group
2002-03	Member of Council, Cancer Research UK
	Member, Scientific Committee, Cancer Research UK
2002-11	Academic Advisory Board, Asian Institute of Medicine, Science and Technology, Malaysia

PRINCIPAL RESEARCH INTERESTS

Acid-base regulation, lactic acidosis, measurement of cell pH, effects of acid-base disorders on regulation of intermediary metabolism, lactate transport, control of gluconeogenesis and ureagenesis, treatment of acid-base disorders, diabetic ketoacidosis, hepatic heterogeneity and *in situ* mapping of hepatic lobular metabolism, fetal programming of diabetes, disorders of calcium metabolism, hepatic intralobular temperature gradients.

(Work supported by grants principally from the Medical Research Council, but also from the Wellcome Trust, the Department of Health and Action Research).

PUBLICATIONS
(In each section, the entries are in chronological order)

Books

1. R.D. Cohen and H.F. Woods (1976). *"Clinical and Biochemical Aspects of Lactic Acidosis"*, Blackwell, Oxford, pp. 276

2. R.D. Cohen, B. Lewis, K.G.M.M. Alberti and A.M. Denman (Eds.) (1990). "The Metabolic and Molecular Basis of Acquired Disease", Ballière Tindall, London, pp. 2082

3. R.D.Cohen (2011) *"Man and the Liver"*, Matador, Kibworth Beauchamp, Leicestershire,UK, pp.143

4. R.D. Cohen (2012) *"NEPHROSAPIENS – A History of Man's Thinking about the Kidney"*, Kibworth Beauchamp, Leicestershire, UK, pp. 54

5. R.D. Cohen (2012) *"SPLANCREAS – and other offal"*, Matador, Kibworth Beauchamp, Leicestershire, UK, pp.

6. R.D. Cohen (2013) "A *Muscle Odyssey"*, Matador, Kibworth Beauchamp, Leicestershire, UK, pp.

7. R.D. Cohen (2013) *"Skin and Bones"*, Matador, Kibworth Beauchamp, Leicestershire, UK, pp.

8. R.D.Cohen (2013) *CORPUS HOMINIS – "Memoirs of an academic physician"* Matador, Kibworth Beauchamp, Leicestershire, UK

Full Refereed Papers (in chronological order of publication)

W.A.H. Rushton and R.D. Cohen (1954). Visual purple and the course of dark adaptation. *Nature* 173, 301-301

J.M. Ledingham and R.D. Cohen (1962). Circulatory changes during the reversal of experimental hypertension. *Clinical Science* 22, 69-77

R.D. Cohen (1962). Effect on the plasma citrate of treatment of primary hypothyroidism with triiodothyronine. *Nature* 196, 486-487

R.D. Cohen (1963). Water and electrolyte metabolism during the treatment of myxoedema, *Clinical Science* 25, 293-303

J.M. Ledingham and R.D. Cohen (1963). The role of the heart in the pathogenesis of hypertension. *Lancet* ii, 979-981

J.M. Ledingham and R.D. Cohen (1964). Changes in the extracellular fluid volume and cardiac output during the development of experimental renal hypertension. *Canadian Medical Association Journal* 90, 292-294

R.D. Cohen, I.P. Ross and A.D. Dayan (1964). Metabolic studies in a case of adrenocortical hyperfunction associated with carcinoma of the lung. *Journal of Clinical Endocrinology* 24, 401-407

R.D. Cohen and R.E.S. Prout (1964). The origin of urinary citrate. *Clinical Science* 26, 237-241.

R.D. Cohen and R.E.S. Prout (1965). Studies on the renal transport of citrate using ^{14}C-citrate. *Clinical Science* 28, 487-497

R.D. Cohen and H.G. Lloyd-Thomas (1966). Exercise electrocardiogram in myxoedema. *British Medical Journal* ii, 327-330

R.D. Cohen (1966). *Metabolic changes during the treatment of myxoedema.* MD Thesis (Cantab)

R.D. Cohen, B.R. Simpson, L. Strunin and J.M. Strunin (1967). The early effects of infusion of sodium bicarbonate or sodium lactate on intracellular hydrogen ion activity in dogs. *Clinical Science* 33, 233-247

T.M. Savege, B.R. Simpson and R.D. Cohen (1969). Treatment of severe salicylate poisoning by forced alkaline diuresis. *British Medical Journal* i, 35-36

R.D. Cohen and F.P. Vince (1969). Pseudohypoparathyroidism with raised plasma alkaline phosphatase. *Archives of Diseases of Childhood* 44, 96-101

W.D. Walker, F.J. Goodwin and R.D. Cohen (1969). Mean intracellular hydrogen ion activity in the whole body, liver, heart and skeletal muscle of the rat. *Clinical Science* 36, 409-417

D.E. Barnado, R.D. Cohen and R.A. Iles (1970). Idiopathic lactic and beta-hydroxybutyric acidosis. *British Medical Journal* ii, 248-249

F.P. Vince, B.J. Boucher, R.D. Cohen, A.S. Mason and J. Godfrey (1970). The response of plasma sugar, free fatty acids, 11-hydroxycorticosteroids and growth hormone to insulin induced hypoglycaemia in primary myxoedema. *Journal of Endocrinology* 48, 389-400

R.D. Cohen, R.A. Iles, D. Barnett, M.E.O. Howell and J. Strunin (1971). The relationship between lactate uptake and intracellular pH in the isolated perfused rat liver. *Clinical Science* 41, 158-170

R.A. Iles, D. Barnett, L. Strunin, J. Strunin, B.R. Simpson and R.D. Cohen (1972). The effect of hypoxia on succinate metabolism in man and the isolated perfused dog liver. *Clinical Science* 42, 35-45

R.D. Cohen, J.D. Ward, T.M. Savege, A.J.S. Brain, C.R. Murray and R.A. Iles(1973),The relationship between phenformin therapy and lactic acidosis. *Diabetologia* 9, 43-46

M.H. Lloyd, R.A. Iles, J. Strunin, O. Layton, B.R. Simpson and R.D. Cohen (1973). The relationship between intracellular pH and lactate metabolism in the isolated perfused rat liver in simulated metabolic acidosis, *Clinical Science* 45, 543-549

P. Belchetz, M.H. Lloyd, R.G.S. Johns and R.D. Cohen (1973). Effect of late-night calcium supplements on overnight urinary calcium excretion in pre- and postmenopausal women. *British Medical Journal* 2, 510-512

B.J. Boucher, R.D. Cohen, R.J. Frankel, A.S. Mason and B. Broadley (1973). Partial and total lipodystrophy: changed in circulating sugar, free fatty acids, insulin and growth hormone following the administration of glucose and of insulin. *Clinical Endocrinology* 2, 111-126

R.A. Iles and R.D. Cohen (1974). The effect of varying the amount of unlabelled 5,5-dimethyloxazolidine-2,4-dione (DMO) in the measurement of rat hepatic intracellular pH using ^{14}C-DMO. *Clinical Science and Molecular Medicine* 46, 277-280

M.H. Lloyd, R.A. Iles, B. Walton, C.A. Hamilton and R.D. Cohen (1975). Effect of phenformin on gluconeogenesis from lactate and intracellular pH in the isolated perfused guinea pig liver, *Diabetes* 24, 618-624

B.J. Boucher, R.D. Cohen, M.W. France and A.S. Mason (1975). Plasma free fatty acid turnover in total lipodystrophy, *Clinical Endocrinology* 4, 83-88

C.O. Record, R.A. Iles, R.D. Cohen and R. Williams (1975). Acid-base and metabolic disturbances in fulminant hepatic failure, *Gut* 16, 144-149

D.R. Corless, M. Beer, B.J. Boucher, S.P. Gupta and R.D.Cohen (1975). Vitamin D status in long-stay geriatric patients, *Lancet* ii, 1404-1406

J. Yudkin and R.D. Cohen (1975). The contribution of the kidney to the removal of a lactic acid load under normal and acidotic conditions in the conscious rat. *Clinical Science and Molecular Medicine* 28, 131-131

J. Yudkin and R.D. Cohen (1976). The effect of acidosis on lactate removal by the perfused rat kidney, *Clinical Science and Molecular Medicine* 50, 185-194

J. Yudkin, R.D. Cohen and B. Slack (1976). The haemodynamic effects of metabolic acidosis in the rat. *Clinical Science and Molecular Medicine* 50, 177-184

D.V. Morris, M. Beer, N.D. Carter, B.J. Boucher and R.D. Cohen (1976). Rapid diagnosis of thyroid disease using carbonic anhydrase immunoassay, *Lancet* iv, 1385-1387

P.E. Belchetz, R.D. Cohen, J.L.H. O'Riordan and S. Tomlinson (1976). Factitious hypercalcaemia, *British Medical Journal* 1, 690-691

B. Barber, R.D. Cohen, D.J. Kenny, J. Rowson and M. Scholes (1976). Some problems of confidentiality in medical computing, *Journal of Medical Ethics* 2, 71-73

B. Barber, R.D. Cohen and M. Scholes (1976). A review of The London Hospital computer project, *Medical Informatics* 1, 61-72

J.M. Barragry, N.D. Carter, M. Beer, M.W. France, J. Auton, B.J. Boucher and R.D. Cohen (1977). Vitamin-D metabolism in nephrotic syndrome, *Lancet* iii, 639-632

R.A. Iles, R.D. Cohen, A.H. Rist and P.G. Barton (1977). The mechanism of inhibition by acidosis of gluconeogenesis from lactate in rat liver. *Biochemical Journal* 164, 185-191

P.G. Baron, R.A. Iles and R.D. Cohen (1978). Effect of varying PCO_2 on intracellular pH and lactate consumption in the isolated perfused rat liver. *Clinical Science and Molecular Medicine* 55, 175-181

R.A. Iles, P.G. Baron and R.D Cohen (1978). Mechanism of the effect of varying PCO_2 on gluconeogenesis from lactate in the perfused rat liver. Clinical Science and *Molecular Medicine* 55, 183-188

J.M. Barragry, M.W. France, D. Corless, S.P. Gupta, S. Switala, B.J. Boucher and R.D. Cohen (1978). Intestinal cholecalciferol absorption in the elderly and in younger adults. *Clinical Science and Molecular Medicine* 55, 213-220

D. Corless, S. Switala, B.J. Boucher, S.P.Gupta, J.M. Barragry, R.D. Cohen and B.L. Diffey (1978). Response of plasma 25-hydroxyvitamin D to ultraviolet irradiation in long-stay geriatric patients. *Lancet* iii, 649- 651

R.A. Iles, P.G. Baron and R.D. Cohen (1979). The effect of reduction of perfusion rate on lactate and oxygen uptake, glucose output and energy supply in the isolated perfused liver of starved rats. *Biochemical Journal* 184, 635-642

J.M. Barragry, M.W. France, B.J. Boucher and R.D. Cohen (1979). Metabolism of Intravenously administered cholecalciferol in man. *Clinical Endocrinology* 11, 491-495

R.G. Long, J.M. Barragry, P. Mitchenere, M.S. Beer, B.J. Boucher and R.D. Cohen.(1980). Effect of conjugated and unconjugated hyperbilirubinaemia on the plasma 25-hydroxyvitamin D response to ultraviolet radiation in the rat, *Clinical Science* 59, 293-296

R.A. Iles, R.D. Cohen and P.G. Baron (1981). The effect of combined ischaemia and acidosis on lactate uptake and gluconeogenesis in the perfused rat liver, *Clinical Science* 60, 537-542

R.A. Iles, R.D. Cohen, P.G. Baron, J.A. Smith and R.M. Henderson (1981). The effect of adrenaline on hepatic lactate uptake in the acidotic partially ischaemic rat liver *Clinical Science* 60, 543-548

J.P. Monson, J.A. Smith., R.D. Cohen and R.A. Iles. Lactate entry into isolated rat hepatocytes: evidence for a transporter. *Biochemical Society Transactions* 9, 401-402, 1981

J.P. Monson, J.A. Smith, R.D. Cohen and R.A. Iles (1982). Evidence for a lactate transporter in the plasma membrane of the rat hepatocyte. *Clinical Science* 62, 441-420

R.D. Cohen, R.M. Henderson, R.A. Iles and J. Smith (1982). Metabolic interrelationships of intracellular pH measured by double-barrelled micro-electrodes in perfused rat liver. *Journal of Physiology (Lond)* 330, 69-80

K.C. Ng, P.A. Revell, M. Beer, B.J. Boucher, R.D. Cohen and H.L.F. Currey (1984). Incidence of metabolic bone disease in rheumatoid arthritis and osteoarthritis. *Annals of the Rheumatic Diseases* 43, 370-377

N.D.T. Martin, G.J.A.I. Snodgrass and R.D. Cohen (1984). Idiopathic infantile hypercalcaemia – a continuing enigma, *Archives of Disease in Childhood* 59, 605-613

S.G. Welch, H.K. Metcalfe, J.P. Monson, R.D. Cohen, R.M. Henderson and R.A. Iles (1984). L(+) lactate binding to preparations of rat hepatocyte plasma membranes, *Journal of Biological Chemistry* 259, 15264-15271

J.P. Monson, R.M. Henderson, J.A. Smith, M. Faus-Dader, N.D. Carter, R. Heath, H. Metcalfe and R.D. Cohen (1984). The mechanism of inhibition of ureogenesis by acidosis. *Bioscience Reports* 4, 819-825

P.J.T. Drew, J.P. Monson, H.K. Metcalfe, S.J.W. Evans, R.A. Iles and R.D. Cohen (1985). The effect of arginine vasopressin on ureagenesis in isolated rat hepatocytes. *Clinical Science* 69, 231-233

N.D.T. Martin, G.J.A.I. Snodgrass, R.D. Cohen, C.E. Porteous, R.D. Coldwell, D.J.Trafford and H.L.J. Makin (1985). Vitamin D metabolites in idiopathic infantile hypercalcaemia. *Archives of Diseases of* Childhood 60, 1140-1143

H.K. Metcalf., J.P. Monson., P.J. Drew., R.A. Iles., N.D. Carter and R.D. Cohen. Inhibition of gluconeogenesis and urea synthesis in isolated rat hepatocytes by acetazolamide. *Biochemical Society Transactions* 13, 255, 1985

D. Corless, E. Dawson, F. Fraser, M. Ellis, S.J.W. Evans, J.D. Perry, C. Reisner, C.P. Silver, M. Beer, B.J. Boucher and R.D. Cohen (1985). Do vitamin D supplements improve the physical capabilities of elderly patients? *Age and Ageing* 14, 76-84

H.K. Metcalfe, J.P. Monson, S.G. Welch and R.D. Cohen (1986). Inhibition of lactate removal by ketone bodies in rat liver: evidence for a quantitatively important role of the plasma membrane lactate transporter in lactate metabolism, *Journal of Clinical Investigation* 78, 743-747

P.J.T. Drew, J.P. Monson, H.K. Metcalfe, S.J.W. Evans, R.A. Iles and R.D. Cohen (1985) The effect of arginine vasopressin on ureagenesis in isolated rat hepatocytes. *Clinical Science* 69, 231-233

H.K. Metcalfe, J.P. Monson, S.G. Welch and R.D. Cohen (1986). Carrier-mediated efflux of ketone bodies in isolated rat hepatocytes, *Clinical Science* 71, 755-761

R.M. Henderson, P.B. Bell, R.D. Cohen, C. Browning and R.A. Iles (1986). Measurement of intracellular pH in rat kidney in vivo. *American Journal of Physiology* 250, F203-F209

H.K. Metcalfe, J.P.Monson, R.D. Cohen and C. Padgham (1988). Enhanced carrier-mediated lactate entry into isolated hepatocytes from starved and diabetic rats. *Journal of Biological Chemistry* 263, 19505-19509

G.A. Hitman, L. Garde, W. Daoud, G.J.A.I. Snodgrass and R.D. Cohen (1989). The calcitonin-CGRP gene in the infantile hypercalcaemia/Williams-Beuren syndrome, *Journal of Medical Genetics* 26, 609-613

J.S. Beech, S.R. Williams, R.D. Cohen and R.A. Iles (1989). Gluconeogenesis and the protection of hepatic intracellular pH during diabetic ketoacidosis in rats. *Biochemical Journal* 263, 737-744

M.K. Almond, A. Smith, R.D. Cohen and G. Flynn (1991). Substrate and pH effects on glutamine synthesis in rat liver: consequences for acid-base regulation. *Biochemical Journal* 178, 709-714

H.K. Metcalfe, J.P. Monson, F. de Allie and R.D. Cohen (1992). Effects of D-3-hydroxybutyrate and acetoacetate on lactate removal in isolated perfused livers from starved and fed rats, *Metabolism* 41, 435-440.

M.K. Almond, R.A. Iles and R.D. Cohen (1992). Hepatic glutamine metabolism and acid-base regulation, *Mineral and Electrolyte Metabolism* 18, 237-240

J.S. Beech, R.A. Iles and R.D. Cohen (1993). Bicarbonate in the treatment of metabolic acidosis: effects on hepatic intracellular pH, gluconeogenesis and lactate disposal in rats, *Metabolism* 42, 341-346

J.S. Beech, K.M. Nolan, R.A. Iles, R.D. Cohen, S.C.R. Williams and S.J.W. Evans (1994). The effects of sodium bicarbonate and a mixture of sodium bicarbonate and sodium carbonate (Carbicarb) on skeletal muscle pH and haemodynamic status in rats with hypovolaemic shock, *Metabolism* 43, 1-7

J.S. Beech, S.C.R. Williams, R.A. Iles, K.M. Nolan, S.J.W. Evans and T.C.D. Going (1995). Hemodynamic and metabolic effects in diabetic ketoacidosis in rats of treatment with sodium bicarbonate or a mixture of sodium bicarbonate and sodium carbonate. *Diabetologia* 38, 889-898

M.A. Staricoff, R.D. Cohen and J.P. Monson (1995). Carrier-mediated lactate entry into isolated hepatocytes from fed and starved rats: zonal distribution and temperature dependence, *Bioscience Reports* 15, 99-109

R.D.Cohen. (1995). New evidence in the bicarbonate controversy. *Applied Cardiopulmonary Pathophysiology* 5, 135-138

S.P. Burns, R.D. Cohen, R.A. Iles, J.P. Germain, T.C.H. Going, S.J.W. Evans and P. Royston (1996). A method for determination in situ of variations within the hepatic lobule of hepatocyte function and metabolite concentrations. *Biochemical Journal* 319, 377- 383

S.P. Burns., M. Desai., R.D. Cohen, C.N. Hales, R.A. Iles, J.P. Germain, T.C.H. Going and R.A. Bailey. (1997). Gluconeogenesis, glucose handling, and structural changes in livers of the adult offspring of rats partially deprived of protein during pregnancy and lactation. *Journal of Clinical Investigation* 100, 1768-1774

S.P. Burns., R.D. Cohen, R.A. Iles, R.A. Bailey, M. Desai, J.P. Germain, T.C.H. Going (1997). Zonation of gluconeogenesis, ketogenesis and intracellular pH in livers from normal and diabetic ketoacidotic rats: evidence for intralobular redistribution of metabolic events in ketoacidosis. *Biochemical Journal* 343, 273-280

S.P.Burns, H.C. Murphy, R.A. Iles, R.A.Bailey, R.D.Cohen. (2000). Hepatic intralobular mapping of fructose metabolism in rat liver. *Biochemical Journal* 349, 539-545

S.P.Burns, H.C. Murphy, R.A. Iles, R.D. Cohen. (2001). Lactate supply as a determinant of the distribution of intracellular pH within the hepatic lobule. *Biochemical Journal* 358, 569-571

H.C.Murphy, G.Regan, I.G.Bogdarina, Clark, A.J.L, Iles, R.A., Cohen, R.D., Hitman, G.A., Berry, C.L., Coade, Z., Petry, C.J., Burns, S.P. (2003). Fetal programming of perivenous glucose uptake reveals a regulatory mechanism governing glucose output during refeeding. *Diabetes* 52, 1326-1332

P.Sasi, S.P.Burns, C. Waruiru, M.English, C.L.Hobson, C.G.King, M.Mosobo, J.S.Beech, R.A.Iles, B.J.Boucher, R.D.Cohen. (2007) Metabolic acidosis and other determinants of hemoglobin-oxygen dissociation in severe childhood *Plasmodium falciparum* malaria. *American Journal of Tropical Medicine and Hygiene* 77, 256-260

R.D. Cohen, C.L. Brown, C. Nickols, P. Levey, B.J. Boucher, S.E. Greenwald, Wen Wang (2011) Inbuilt mechanisms for overcoming functional problems inherent in hepatic microlobular function. *Computational and Mathematical Methods in Medicine* Article ID 185845, 8 pages

R.D. Cohen (2011) A medical problem of cobblestones and pavements. *Quarterly Journal of Medicine* 104, 1011

Selected Chapters and Invited Reviews

R.D. Cohen (1971). Some aspects of metabolic bone disease related to rheumatology. *Rheumatology and Physical Medicine* 11, 162-172

R.D.Cohen, R.A. Iles and M.H. Lloyd (1973). Perfusion of the rat liver. In: "*Isolated Organ Perfusion*", Eds. H.D. Ritchie and J.D. Hardcastle, Staples, London, pp .120-134
R.D. Cohen (1975). Body Fluids. In: "*Clinical Physiology*" 4th edn. Eds. E.J.M. Campbell, C.J. Dickinson and J.D.H. Slater. Blackwell, Oxford, pp. 1-42

R.D. Cohen and B.R. Simpson (1975). Lactate metabolism *Anesthesiology* 43, 661-673

R.D. Cohen and R.A. Iles (1975). Intracellular pH: measurement, control and metabolic interrelationships. *CRC Reviews in the Clinical Laboratory Sciences* 6, 101-143

R.D. Cohen (1976). Disorders of lactic acid metabolism. *Clinics in Endocrinology and Metabolism* 5, 613-625

R.D. Cohen and R.A. Iles (1977). Lactic acidosis: some physiological and clinical considerations, *Clinical Science and Molecular Medicine* 53, 405-410

R.D. Cohen (1978). The production and removal of lactate. In: "*Lactate in Acute Conditions*", Eds. H. Bossart and C. Perret. Karger, Basel, pp.10-19

R.D. Cohen (1978). Prevention and treatment of lactic acidosis. In: "*Topics in Therapeutics (4)*", Ed. D. W. Vere, Pitman, London, pp.191-197

R.D. Cohen (1979). The relative risks of different biguanides in the causation of lactic acidosis. *Research and Clinical Forums* 1(4), 124-134

R.D. Cohen (1979). Evaluation of Computer systems in medicine. (Keynote address) *Proceedings of "Medical Informatics Berlin 1979"*. Eds. B. Barber, F. Gremy, K. Uberla and G. Wagner, Springer Verlag, Berlin, pp.931-937

R.D. Cohen and R.A. Iles (1980). Lactic acidosis: diagnosis and treatment. *Clinics in Endocrinology and Metabolism* 9, 513-937

R.D. Cohen (1980). Metabolic bone disease. In: "*Clinical Rheumatology*" 3rd edn., Ed. H.L.F. Currey. Pitman, London, pp. 251-264

R.D. Cohen (1981). Computing in the National Health Service. *Royal Society of Health Journal* 101, 174-278

R.D. Cohen (1980). The prevention and treatment of Type B lactic acidosis. *British Journal of Hospital Medicine* June, 1980, 577-581

R.D. Cohen, R.M. Henderson, R.A. Iles, J.P. Monson and J.A. Smith (1982). The techniques and uses of intracellular pH measurements. In: "*Metabolic Acidosis*", (Ciba Foundation Symposium No. 97), pp. 20-35

R.D. Cohen (1982). Some acid problems (Bradshaw Lecture, The Royal College of Physicians of London), *Journal of the Royal College of Physicians of London* 16, 69-77

G. Waldron, S.I. Cohen and R.D. Cohen (1982). Psychiatric aspects of metabolic, endocrine and autoimmune disease. In: "*Medicine and Psychiatry – Practical Approach*", Eds. F. Creed and J.M. Pfeffer, Pitman, London, pp.430-452

R.D. Cohen and H.F.Woods (1983). Lactic acidosis revisited. *Diabetes* 32, 181-191

R.D. Cohen and H.F.Woods (1981). Disturbances of acid-base homeostasis. In: "*Oxford Textbook of Medicine*", 1ˢᵗ edn., Eds. D.J. Weatherall, J.G.G. Ledingham and D.A. Warrell, Oxford University Press, pp. 9.116 -9.126.

R.D. Cohen (1984). Body Fluids. In: "*Clinical Physiology*", 5th. edn., Eds. E.J.M. Campbell, C.J. Dickinson, J.D.H. Slater, C.R.W. Edwards and E.K. Sikora, Blackwell, Oxford, pp.1-40

R.D. Cohen (1986). Computers in medical administration, record linkage and storage, patient management and research. In: "*The Oxford Companion to Medicine*", Eds. J. Walton, P.B. Beeson and R. Bodley Scott, Vol. 1, pp.251-254

R.D. Cohen (1986). Metabolic bone disease. In: "Clinical Rheumatology", 4th edn., Ed. H.L.F. Currey, Pitman, London, pp.301-315

R.D. Cohen (1986). The role of the liver in acid-base disorders. In: "*Advanced Medicine*", Vol. 21, Ed. M.J. Brown, Churchill Livingstone, London, pp.201 210

R.A. Iles and R.D. Cohen (1987). NMR as a metabolic tool. *Clinical Endocrinology and Metabolism* 1, 937-966

R.D. Cohen (1983). Pathophysiology of lactic acidosis. In: "*Update in Intensive Care and Emergency Medicine*", Vol. 5, Ed. J. L. Vincent, Springer Verlag, pp.40-43

Metcalfe HK, Monson JP, Welch SG, Bell PB and Cohen RD. Reciprocal inhibition of lactate and 3-hydroxybutyrate binding to rat hepatocyte membranes and inhibition of lactate transport into isolated rat hepatocytes by 3-hydroxybutyrate. In: *Carrier-mediated transport of solutes from blood to tissue*. Eds. Yudilevitch DL and Mann GE. Longman, New York and London, 1985. pp. 345-348

R.D. Cohen and W.G. Guder (1988). Carbohydrate metabolism and pH. In: "*pH Homeostasis*". Ed. D. Häussinger, Academic Press, London, pp.403-426

R.D. Cohen and H.F. Woods (1988). Disorders of acid-base homeostasis. In: "*Oxford Textbook of Medicine*", 2nd edn., Eds. D.J. Weatherall, J.G.G. Ledingham and D.A. Warrell, Oxford University Press, pp.9.164-9.175

R.D. Cohen (1988). Renal tubular acidosis. In: "*Oxford Textbook of Medicine*", 2nd edn. Eds. D.J. Weatherall, J.G.G. Ledingham and D.A. Warrell, Oxford University Press, pp.18.171-18.174

R.D. Cohen (1989). The pathophysiology of lactic acidosis. *Applied Cardiopulmonary Pathophysiology* 2, 285-291

R.D. Cohen (1989). Should bicarbonate be used in the treatment of metabolic acidosis? *Debates in Medicine 3*, 202-120

R.D. Cohen (1990). Disorders of acid-base regulation. In: "*Metabolic and Molecular Basis of Acquired Disease*", Eds. R.D. Cohen, B. Lewis, K.G.M.M. Alberti and A.M. Denman. Baillière Tindall, London, pp.962-1001.

R.D. Cohen (1990). Lactic acidosis: pathophysiology and therapeutic problems. In: "*Proceedings of 5th World Congress on Intensive and Critical Care Medicine*" Kyoto, Japan, Elsevier, Amsterdam, pp. 97-10.

R.D. Cohen (1991). pH and carbohydrate metabolism. In: "*Encyclopedia of Human Biology*". Academic Press, Vol. 5, 821-828

R.D. Cohen (1991). Roles of the liver and kidney in acid-base regulation and its disorders. *British Journal of Anaesthesia* 67, 154-164

R.D. Cohen (1991). The significance of cell pH changes in metabolic acidosis. *Applied Cardiopulmonary Physiology* 3, 313-317

R.D. Cohen (1991). A reassessment of the pathogenesis of diabetic ketoacidosis. In: *Horizons in Medicine* No. 3, Eds. C.A. Seymour and J.A. Summerfield, pp. 342-349.

R.D. Cohen., Beech. J.S., R.A. Iles. A reassessment of the pathogenesis of diabetic ketoacidosis. In: *Horizons in Medicine*. Vol.3. Eds. Seymour, C.A., Summerfield, J.A. Transmedica Europe Limited, Cambridge University Press. pp. 342-350

R.D. Cohen (1992). Clinical implications of the pathophysiology of lactic acidosis: The role of defects in lactate disposal. In: *"Hypoxia, metabolic acidosis and the circulation"*. Ed. A. I. Arieff, Oxford University Press, pp.85-98

R.D. Cohen (1992). Essential Population-Based Competencies for Undergraduate and Postgraduate Medical Students. In *"The Medical School's Mission and the Population's Health"*. Eds. White, K.L., Connelly, J.E. Springer-Verlag, New York.

R.D. Cohen (1994). Lactic acidosis – new perspective on origins and treatment. *Diabetes Reviews* 2, 86-96

R.D. Cohen (1995). The Liver and Acid-Base Regulation. In *"Fluid, Electrolyte and Acid-Base Disorders"*. 2nd Ed. Arieff A.I., DeFronzo, R.A. Churchill Livingstone, New York. Ch.15 pp. 777-790

R.D. Cohen and H.F.Woods (1996) Disturbances of acid-base homeostasis. In: *"Oxford Textbook of Medicine"*, 3rd edn, Eds. D.J. Weatherall, J.G.G. Ledingham and D.A. Warrell, Oxford University Press, pp. 1533-154.

R.D. Cohen (1996) The renal tubular acidoses. In: *"Oxford Textbook of Medicine"*, 3rd edn., Eds. D.J. Weatherall, J.G.G. Ledingham and D.A. Warrell, Oxford University Press, pp. 1533-1544

R.D. Cohen (1997). Acid-base abnormalities. In *"Textbook of Intensive Care"*. Eds. Goldhill, D.R. Withington, P.S. Chapman and Hall, London pp. 125-133

S.P. Burns, R.D. Cohen, R.A. Iles. (1997). Mapping of hepatic acinar function and metabolite concentration. In: *"Advances in Hepatic Encephalopathy and Metabolism in Liver Disease"*. Eds. Record, C., Al-Mardini, H. Newcastle Ipswich. Ch. 2 pp. 11-16

R.D. Cohen. pH and Carbohydrate Metabolism. In: *Encyclopedia of Human Biology*, New York: Academic Press, 1991, pp. 821-828

R.D. Cohen and H.F.Woods (2007) Disturbances of acid-base homeostasis. In *"Oxford Textbook of Medicine"*, 4th edn, Eds. D.A. Warrell, T.M.Cox, J.D.Firth. Oxford University Press, Vol. 2 pp. 139-149

R.D. Cohen and H.F.Woods (2010) Disturbances of acid-base homeostasis. In: *"Oxford Textbook of Medicine"*, 5th edn. Eds. D.A. Warrell, T.M.Cox, J.D.Firth Oxford University Press Vol. 2 pp. 1738-1751

Selected letters
Comment on Nyirenda SJ, Dean S, Lyons V, Chapman KE Diabetologia 49, 1412 – 1420, 2006 and on McCurdy CE, Friedman JE *Diabetologia* 49, 1338 -1141, 2006 (fetal programming issues). Letter published *Diabetologi*a 49, 2809-2810, 2006

Comment on Huxley R. Fatal flaw in the fetal argument *British Journal of Nutrition*. 95, 441- 442, 2006. Letter published in *British Journal of Nutrition* 96, 1169, 2006.

Glossary

In the text, a glossary entry is indicated by an asterisk (*). Although many of the glossary entries are explained at the first time of mention, the explanations are repeated here, on the assumption that the reader will have forgotten the explanation by the time he or she reaches the term again!

Acetylation/deacetylation – the addition or removal of acetyl groups.

Acidosis – a condition where the blood is more acid than normal, or has a tendency to become so.

Alkalosis – a condition where the blood is more alkaline than normal, or has a tendency to become so.

Auto-immune disease – the general name given to a group of conditions in which the body's immune system makes antibodies against its own organs.

Beth Din – The Hebrew for 'House of Judgement'. It is now concerned mainly with the interpretation and promulgation of Jewish religious law.

Bubonic plague – a condition caused by infection with the organism *Pasteurella pestis*, responsible for numerous epidemics. Named after the discoverer of the organism, Louis Pasteur.

Coprolalia – continuous vocalisation of obscenities (literally 'faeces speaking').

Cystine – an amino-acid in which two cysteine molecules are joined by the sulphur atoms.

Cystitis – inflammation of the bladder, causing a frequent desire to pass urine, and pain whilst doing so.

DNA methylation – addition of a methyl group to either the cytosine or adenine bases of the DNA molecule. This typically silences the expression of genes.

Emetic – a drug or medicine which produces vomiting.

Endocrine glands – these glands secrete hormones into the blood stream, to influence the function of other body structures. They contrast with exocrine glands, which secrete their product in to a duct, and thence to where the product is required (e.g. salivary glands).

Eosinophilia – a large number of the class of white cells in the blood known as eosinophils. They are concerned with mediating allergic responses, and may be involved in conditions such as asthma.

Erysipelas – an acute infection of the skin caused by *Streptococcus pyogenes*.

Expectorant – a medicine which aids the coughing up of sputum.

Fibrinogen – a protein component of the clotting mechanism; it is converted during the process of clotting into fibrin, an essential component of the clot, and therefore crucial in homeostasis.

Fourier transformation – a mathematical technique by which the graphical tracing of a process may be resolved into a series of frequencies.

Glomerulonephritis – an inflammatory disease of the kidneys, due to auto – immune processes, primarily affecting the glomeruli of the renal tubules.

Glucokinase – an enzyme present in liver and pancreas which adds a phosphate moiety to glucose, producing glucose 6-phosphate.

Gluconeogenesis – the metabolic pathway of formation of glucose from various precursors, e.g. certain amino-acids.

Gonorrhoea – a venereal disease caused by the bacterium *Neisseria gonorrhoeae*.

Herpes Zoster – a viral infection of the cells of the sensory nerves, causing a blistering and often painful eruption. The lay term is 'shingles'.

Histone acetylation/deacetylation – histones are globular proteins around which DNA strands are wound. Acetylation of histones is associated with activation of transcription of DNA into RNA, and deacetylation with reduction of such activity.

Hypothermia – a low body temperature

Kashrut – the whole gamut of rules determining whether a food item is, or is not, Kosher

Kosher – this is the term applied to an item of diet, in which the animal has been killed in a prescribed fashion (cutting of the throat). Some foods are inherently 'not Kosher', e.g. pigs, because of the association with trichiniasis, or horses, because they do not have cloven hooves, and sea-food, such as lobster and prawns.

Kussmaul breathing – deep sighing respiration, typically seen in cases of acidosis in which the respiratory centre is stimulating respiration in an attempt to correct the acidosis by getting rid of carbon dioxide.

Left ventricular ejection fraction – the fraction of the volume of blood contained by the left ventricle in diastole which is ejected into the aorta during systole.

Leishmaniasis – disease caused by parasites of the genus *Leishmania*, transmitted by the bite of the sandfly.

Micturition – the act of passing urine.

Multiple sclerosis – a common and disabling demyelinating disease.

Mikvah – a ritual bath taken by orthodox Jewish women during menstruation.

Myelin – the insulating material contained in the myelin sheaths of nerve fibres, produced by the surrounding cells (Schwann cells). It contains complexes of proteins and fats (glycolipids, principally galactocerebroside).

Nodes of Ranvier – short intervals between the segments of myelinated nerves, in which the nerve plasma membrane is uninsulated and thus allows the nerve impulse to jump from one node to the next, thereby greatly increasing the speed of conduction of the nerve impulse.

Onchocerciasis – (otherwise known as River Blindness). A disease transmitted by the bite of the blackfly, which injects in its saliva the parasite *Wolbachia pipientis*; the latter are carried in the blood stream to many organs, including the eyes, where they set up an inflammatory response.

Ophthalmoscope – a hand held instrument for inspecting the internal structures of the eye.

Osmosis – the process by which in a system containing two aqueous solutions of substances separated by a membrane permeable only to water, the water moves from the solution of lower concentration to that of the higher.

Parathyroid glands – these are small *endocrine glands, situated two on each side of the trachea, underneath the thyroid gland. They secrete parathormone, a protein hormone, which raises the plasma calcium level and lowers the plasma phosphate level.

pH – the negative logarithm to the base 10 of the hydrogen ion concentration; a standard measure of acidity and alkalinity of solutions. A pH of 7.0 represents neutrality, lower values being acid, and higher values being alkaline.

Prostatectomy – surgical removal of the prostate gland, which is done either by making an abdominal incision through the bladder wall, or with an instrument inserted through the penis.

Proton – a hydrogen ion (H^+).

Pyruvate carboxylase – an enzyme which converts pyruvate into oxaloacetate, an intermediate of the tricarboxylic acid cycle.

Renal – pertaining to the kidney.

Renin – a protein hormone formed in the specialised cells of the renal glomerulus, a network of capillaries through which the plasma element of blood is filtered as the first step in the production of urine. Renin has at least two functions, vasoconstriction, and, via a more complex pathway, the stimulation of the cortex of the adrenal glands to produce aldosterone, a hormone which acts on the renal tubules to promote reabsorption of sodium and excretion of potassium ions in the urine.

Respiration – this term has two separate meanings, according to context. It may refer to the act of breathing, or to the metabolic processes of energy generation e.g. in the form of ATP.

Sarcoidosis – this condition is characterised by small lesions in many organs, consisting of lymphocytes, macrophages and giant cells, similar to those seen in tuberculosis, but no tubercle bacilli are present. The giant cells may contain curious inclusions, known as asteroid and Schaumann bodies. A high level of blood calcium may occur, since the macrophages convert vitamin D to its active forrn, 1,25-dihydroxycholecalciferol, without any of the regulation according to need that occurs in the kidneys.

Saltatory conduction – the mode of nerve conduction in which the impulse jumps from one *Node of Ranvier to the next, thereby greatly increasing the speed of conduction.

Shingles – a lay term for herpes zoster.

Stereospecificity – many organic compounds exist in two forms, which are mirror images of each other. Such forms are designated by the prefixes D and L, according to the direction in which a crystal of the compound rotates the plane of polarised light. Most enzymes are stereospecific, i.e. they will only catalyse reactions of one of the two forms of the compound (commonly the L-form in mammalian biology).

Systemic lupus erythematosus – a disease in which the body's immune system is directed against itself; it may affect almost all organs in the body.

Syphilis – a venereal disease caused by *Treponema pallidum.*

Thallium – a metallic element of atomic weight 204.39. Chemical symbol – Tl.

Thymus gland – this gland is located behind the sternum. One of its principle functions is to educate T-lymphocytes, as to which cells to attack and which to leave alone. The leaving alone is the basis of the phenomenon of immune tolerance, which gets disturbed in auto-immune disease.

Transport – term referring to the passage of substances across the cell membrane – either into the cell or out of it. It may be passive, requiring no energy input, i.e. down a concentration and/or charge gradient, or active i.e. up such gradients and requiring input of energy, commonly derived from ATP.

Tubular – adjective referring to the renal tubules which connect the *glomeruli to the bladder.

Ulcerative colitis – a chronic inflammatory disease of the colon, causing bloody diarrhoea and with complications affecting several other organs of the body

Appendix

For simplicity, we deal firstly with heat transfer in a hypothetical lobule in which no mechanisms such as those suggested above in relation to UCP-2 and TRPv4 had evolved. Assume that the lobules are on average spherical, and, in the first place, that heat generation within the lobule is uniform. Let q be the rate of heat production per unit volume of tissue (units $J/(m^3 \text{ sec})$), s the specific heat of tissue, i.e. heat required to raise the temperature of a unit volume of tissue by 1 degree K ($J/(m^3 K)$), k the thermal conductivity ($J/(m \text{ sec K})$). T and u are temperature (in degrees K) and blood velocity (m/sec) respectively at a radial distance r from the centre of the spherical lobule. The general equation of heat transfer is:

$$\nabla \left(-k\nabla T + us\,T\right) = q - s\,\frac{dT}{dt}$$

where ∇ denotes spatial gradient and t is time. For steady state situations considered in this analysis, $dT/dt = 0$, hence:

$$(k\,T + us\,T) = q$$

Assume that diffusive heat transfer is negligible compared with convective heat transfer by the blood flowing down the sinusoids. This is intuitively likely to be the case, because of the high blood flow through the liver. The diffusive term kET can thus be neglected, giving:

$$(us\,T) = q$$

Using Gauss' Theorem, this leads to:

$$\iint_{Surface} us\,T\,dA = \iiint_{Volume} q\,dV$$

i.e. heat flux $(us\,T)$ over the entire surface of a volume in the sphere equals the total heat production in that volume. Integration between r and the surface of the sphere, a, leads to (note that blood flow is in the $-r$ direction):

$$s[r^2 u_r T - a^2 u_a T_a] = q(a^3 - r^3)/3$$

where T_a and u_a are the temperature and average inflow blood velocity at the surface of the sphere. With volume conservation for the blood flow, i.e. $r^2 u_r = a^2 u_a$, the temperature distribution within the spherical lobule can be expressed as:

$$T = T_a + (Vq/Fs)[1 - (r/a)^3] \quad (1)$$

where $V = 4\pi a^3/3$ (the volume of a hepatic lobule) and $F = 4\pi a^2 u_a$ (the volume flow rate of blood entering each lobule). The total temperature difference between the core $(r = 0)$ and the surface $(r = a)$ of the lobule is Vq/Fs.

T_a may reasonably be assumed to be the temperature of the blood supply to the liver; in the case of the perfused liver this is the temperature at which the perfusion system is kept – e.g. 37°C. In the intact animal, this will be the core temperature. The specific heat of tissue, s is taken as 3570 J/(kg K) based on a linear interpolation of results by Haemmericha et al[5] . In man, the volume of a hepatic lobule is approximately 0.179 mm^3 (for a = 0.35 mm) and the average volume flow rate of blood into each lobule is approximately 0.1 mm^3/min, based on a whole liver of 1.5 litre in volume receiving 0.83 litres of blood per minute[6], assuming body surface area 1.73 m^2. The rate of hepatic heat production (q = 30.75 J/(litre.sec)) employed in the present calculations is based on the mean value of 0.41 W per kg body weight, obtained in the anaesthetised dog by Baconnier et al[7]. It assumes that liver accounts for 1/50th of the body weight and that hepatocytes occupy two-thirds of the volume of the liver (i.e. $q = 0.41 \times 50 \times (3/2)$). The temperature distribution derived from this model could then be compared with that directly measured, if this eventually becomes feasible. Fig.1 shows the radial distribution of temperature given by Eqn 1, using the above values for the variables; it indicates that the total theoretical temperature rise on moving from the periphery to the centre of the lobule is approximately 0.9 K.

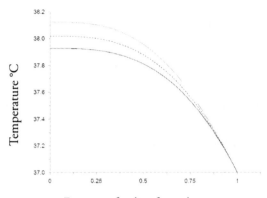

Fraction of radius from the centre

Figure 1. Temperature distribution in the hepatic lobule at different radial distances from the centre, as predicted in the model in the absence of UCP-2. The solid line ($Q_{10}= 1$) is for when heat production rate is constant. The dashed line ($Q_{10}= 3$) and the dotted line ($Q_{10}= 5$) are for when there are temperature-sensitive heat production rates.

Now consider an alternative situation, also in the absence of UCP-2 effects, in which heat production q varies along the radius of the hepatic lobule as a function of the local temperature, so:

$$q(r) = + T(r)$$

where α and β.are constant parameters, given by:

$$\alpha = [(47 -37R)/10]q_a \text{ and } \beta = [(R – 1)/10]q_a$$

Here, R is the increase in heat generation rate per $10°K$ rise in temperature.

In spherical coordinates, the governing equation becomes:

$$1/r^2 . d/dr (r^2u_r sT) = \alpha + \beta T$$
(note that u is in the $– r$ direction)

With volume conservation of blood flow, i.e. $r^2u_r = a^2u_a$, we can separate variables, r and T in the above equation:

$1/(\alpha + \beta T). \; dT = -(r^2)/a^2 u_a s.dr$

Integration of both sides of the equation leads to:

$T_r = \exp [- \beta r^3/3a^2 u_a s)] - (\alpha/\beta)$

With the boundary condition at $r = a$, we have:

$T_r = [T_a + (\alpha/\beta)] \exp[(V\beta/Fs). \{1 - (r/a)^3\}] - (\alpha/\beta)$

The temperature difference between the centre and the surface of the lobule is

$[T_a + (\alpha/\beta)]. \exp[(V\beta/Fs) -1]$ ....(2)

Fig. 1 also shows the temperature distribution with Q_{10} = 3, 4 and 5 (Q_{10} is the factor by which heat production q is increases per $10°K$ temperature rise. There is $0.21 \rightarrow 0.84°K$ increase in temperature difference between the periphery and centre of the lobule compared with the situation when heat production is uniform throughout the lobule.

Index